Essential

Director

OTHER ECONOMIST BOOKS

Guide to Analysing Companies
Guide to Business Modelling
Guide to Economic Indicators
Guide to the European Union
Guide to Financial Markets
Guide to Management Ideas
Numbers Guide
Style Guide

Business Ethics
China's Stockmarket
Economics
E-Commerce
E-Trends
Globalisation
Measuring Business Performance
Successful Innovation
Successful Mergers
Wall Street

Dictionary of Business
Dictionary of Economics
International Dictionary of Finance

Essential Finance
Essential Internet
Essential Investment

Pocket Asia
Pocket Europe in Figures
Pocket World in Figures

The
Economist

Essential

Director

Bob Tricker

THE ECONOMIST IN ASSOCIATION WITH
PROFILE BOOKS LTD

Published by Profile Books Ltd
58A Hatton Garden, London EC1N 8LX

Designed and typeset in EcoType by MacGuru Ltd
info@macguru.org.uk

Printed in Italy by Legoprint – S.p.a. – Lavis (TN)

A CIP catalogue record for this book is available
from the British Library

ISBN 1 86197 560 0

Contents

Preface

There have been some profound changes in the world's board-rooms in the past decade. Many boards are smaller, more professional and better run. Some directors are better informed and more aware of their responsibilities. More independent non-executive directors are involved in regulating as well as de-veloping the future of their company. Audit committees and re-muneration committees are commonplace.

However, most directors still have no training for the job and many have yet to face up to the new expectations of better di-rector performance and improved board effectiveness. In-vestors, both individual and institutional, are making more demands on companies for transparency and disclosure. The in-vestigative media have become even more interested in corpor-ate affairs. The threats of litigation against directors for alleged lapses of fiduciary duty are multiplying. So the need for direc-tors to be informed, up to date and fully aware of their respon-sibilities has never been greater.

The world of corporate governance has changed fundamen-tally since the turn of the century. The bursting of the dotcom bubble left many unanswered questions about the governance of entrepreneurial companies. WorldCom became the world's largest bankruptcy as a result of fraud and board failure. The collapse of Enron led to new corporate governance regulation and law in the United States. And the disintegration of Ander-sen, one of the world's big five accountancy firms, underlined the need for rethinking auditor independence. Non-executive directors lacking independence, financial analysts giving biased advice and senior directors rewarding themselves richly as their companies failed were among other scandals that came to the fore. The post-Enron world of corporate governance is a chal-lenging place. I hope that this book will provide a map of that world that is both informative and entertaining.

Bob Tricker
January 2003

Introduction

Corporate entities are the most important organisations in modern society. They satisfy market needs, provide employment and create wealth. Their actions affect the lives of everyone – whether as customers, employees, suppliers, investors, or in society at large. Given the significance of companies, they clearly need sound management. They also need good governance. Governance is different from management. Managers run the enterprise; the directors ensure that it is being run well and run in the right direction. Governance is the work of the governing body, typically the board of directors.

Questions that this book endeavours to answer are: what does being a director involve, what makes a director effective and what makes for a successful board? The responsibilities, rights, risks and rewards of directorship are also examined, as are the ways power is exercised over companies.

This book is addressed to all who govern organisations – not just companies but also cultural, educational and medical organisations, and charitable and religious societies – and all who have an interest in the way organisations, especially their own, are governed.

The introductory essay provides the basis for a broad understanding of directors' roles, and leads into the extensive A–Z section, which gives practical insights into the work of directors, explores the basis of corporate governance, covers the factors necessary to be a successful director and shows how to build a better board. Cross references given in SMALL CAPITALS make it easy to find related subjects, and the quotations that appear throughout are intended to entertain as well as illuminate. The appendices contain yet more practical help: codes of governance practice, guidelines and checklists for directors and useful websites.

Essential Director is part of a series of *Economist* books that bring clarity to complicated areas of business, finance and management.

Good directors and better boards

Once upon a time a directorship was a sinecure, involving an occasional meeting, some supportive questions, a fee and lunch – but not now. More is expected of directors and members of all governing bodies than ever before, and the difference – positive or negative – directors can make to their companies is arguably greater than ever. The role of a director is crucial, challenging and potentially highly rewarding.

In listed companies, those quoted on the stockmarket, shareholders are no longer compliant. They expect their directors to increase shareholder value, and to do so genuinely, not through accounting distortions and misleading financial disclosure. Institutional investors – insurance companies, pension funds and financial institutions – complain publicly about poor performance, excessive directors' remuneration and other strategic issues, and demand high standards of corporate governance. International credit rating firms also expect high governance standards. Moreover, the demands on listed companies and their directors, from financial regulators and stock exchanges around the world, have increased. The threat of litigation against directors also raises the risk of serious financial exposure and public derision. In the United States, following the Sarbanes-Oxley Act of 2002, the Securities and Exchange Commission (SEC) now requires chief executives (CEOs) and chief financial officers (CFOs) to swear, on oath, that their financial reports omit nothing and contain no untrue statement, on threat of jail.

Directors of private companies (those that are not listed on a stockmarket) do not escape the corporate governance spotlight. The interests of minority shareholders must be protected. In certain circumstances, directors can find themselves personally responsible for their company's debts. They can also be fined heavily if the company fails to meet its statutory obligations. Moreover, shareholders in private companies pay more attention than formerly to standards of corporate governance and the delivery of improvements in their business's performance.

The expectations of society generally have changed too, putting greater emphasis on socially responsible behaviour from companies, again backed by increasing regulation. If the media raise concerns about a company's behaviour, directors can find themselves well and truly in the public eye.

Members of the governing bodies of not-for-profit institutions, such as hospital trusts, colleges, arts and sports organisations and educational bodies, also face demands for good governance. Whether their governing body is called a committee, council, senate, or whatever, its members are expected to act professionally.

Corporate governance is not management

Twenty years ago the phrase "corporate governance" was unfamiliar; today it is commonplace. In the Cadbury Report (1992) corporate governance was defined as the system by which companies are directed and controlled. Boards of directors are responsible for the governance of their companies, ensuring that they are being well run. Managers are responsible for running the enterprise. The shareholders' role in governance is to appoint the directors and the auditors. Poor corporate governance has ruined companies, sent directors to jail, destroyed a global accounting firm and threatened economies and governments.

For years the major focus in business was on management: management schools, management consultants, management gurus. Today the way companies are governed has become more important than the way they are managed – after all, good governance should ensure good management whereas poor governance allows poor management to develop and thrive. Some people fail to make the distinction between governance and management. The board of directors seldom appears on the organisation chart. The idea of management as a hierarchy is commonplace: a chief executive with overall responsibility, heading an organisational pyramid with various managerial levels, delegating authority for management functions downwards and demanding accountability upwards (see Figure 1).

The board, however, is not a hierarchy. Every director has equal responsibility and similar duties and powers. Company law recognises no boss of the board. The work of the board, the

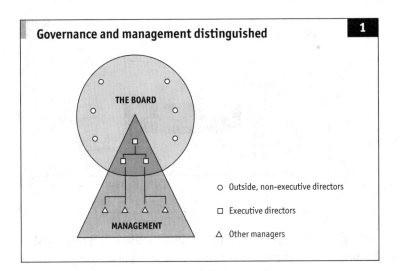

Governance and management distinguished   1

THE BOARD

MANAGEMENT

○ Outside, non-executive directors

□ Executive directors

△ Other managers

governing body of the entity, is shown in Figure 1 as a circle, superimposed on the management. In a unitary board, of course, some directors will also be senior executives, with managerial roles as well as their responsibilities as directors. They are executive directors □ sitting in both the board circle and the management triangle. The other directors, the non-executive or outside directors ○ are members of the board circle but are outside the management hierarchy.

The essential task of directing

The board's task is to direct, which is why directors are so called. The work of the board includes strategy formulation and policymaking, supervision of executive management and accountability to shareholders and others.

In formulating strategy, the board works with senior management, looking ahead in time and outside the firm, seeing it in its strategic environment. Strategies then need to be translated into policies to guide management action and provide plans for subsequent control. The board must also monitor and supervise the activities of executive managers, looking inwards at the current managerial situation and at recent performance. Accountability involves looking outwards and reflecting corporate

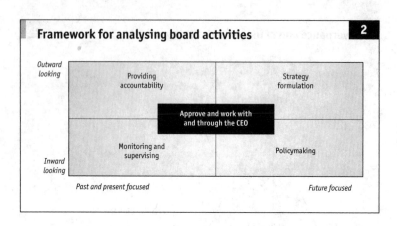

Framework for analysing board activities   2

Outward looking

| Providing accountability | Strategy formulation |

Approve and work with and through the CEO

| Monitoring and supervising | Policymaking |

Inward looking

Past and present focused   Future focused

activities and performance to the shareholders and other stake-holders with legitimate claims to accountability.

Of course, boards vary in the extent to which the board as a whole engages in these functions or delegates work to the CEO and the management team, while ensuring that the necessary monitoring and control processes are in place. Figure 2 provides a simple framework summarising the work of directors.

Figure 2 also highlights an issue for a unitary board, which has both executive and outside directors. The roles in the right-hand boxes – strategy formulation and policymaking – are performance roles, concerned with the board's contribution to corporate direction. Those on the left – executive supervision and accountability – are essentially concerned with ensuring conformance. Figure 3 shows this important distinction. In a two-tier board the roles are separated, with the executive board

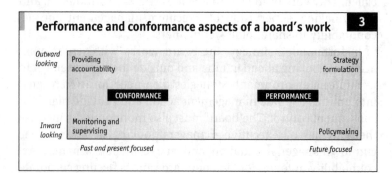

Performance and conformance aspects of a board's work   3

Outward looking

| Providing accountability | Strategy formulation |

CONFORMANCE   PERFORMANCE

| Monitoring and supervising | Policymaking |

Inward looking

Past and present focused   Future focused

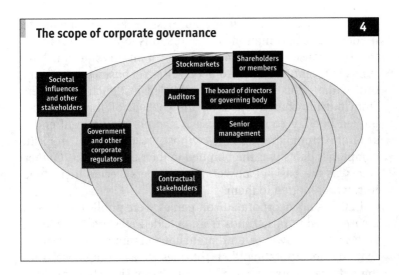

The scope of corporate governance

4

Stockmarkets

Shareholders or members

Societal influences and other stakeholders

Auditors

The board of directors or governing body

Government and other corporate regulators

Senior management

Contractual stakeholders

responsible for performance and the supervisory board responsible for conformance.

The scope of governance

Broadly, corporate governance is about the way power is exercised over corporate entities. Of course, the structure, the membership and the processes of the governing body are central, but relations with shareholders and other sources of finance, the link with independent external auditors, and (in listed companies) the influence of the stockmarket and the financial institutions are fundamental. So are the effects of the company law, the legal institutions and the regulatory mechanisms of the country concerned. Other stakeholders and society at large can also influence corporate governance; Figure 4 provides an overview of its scope.

The developing role of the director

The original concept of the company was immensely innovative, elegantly simple and proved superbly successful. In the middle of the 19th century, apart from companies created by the state or the crown, the only way to do business was as a sole trader or a partnership. If the business became insolvent, the owner could find himself in debtors' prison and his family in the workhouse – hardly an incentive for an investor to risk his funds in a venture run by someone else. Yet businesses growing out of the industrial revolution needed just such investment from outside shareholders. So the concept of the joint stock limited liability company arose – incorporating a legal entity, separate from the owners, whose responsibility for the company's debts was then limited to their equity stake. Ownership was the basis of power. Shareholders elected their directors, who reported to them.

Initially, all incorporated companies were public companies, incorporated to raise funds from outside investors. Early in the 20th century, however, entrepreneurs and family firms realised that, by incorporating their businesses as companies, they limited their personal liability for the business's debts. The private company had arrived.

By the 1930s, many public companies in the United States had outside shareholders, and the separation between owners and management was largely complete. Self-perpetuating boards ruled the companies and did not always act in the best interests of the shareholders. Investors needed protection and so the Securities and Exchange Commission was created.

In the 1970s another governance idea surfaced. Large companies, it was suggested, owed a responsibility not only to their shareholders but also to other stakeholders, such as their employees, customers and suppliers, and even to society. These ideas were, predictably, resisted by directors and debates proved inconclusive. The legal responsibility of boards to be the stewards of their shareholders' interests was maintained.

In Europe, meanwhile, in an attempt to harmonise company law throughout the member states of the European Economic Community, proposals were drafted which would have required all companies in the Community to adopt the German two-tier board model, instead of the unitary board used in American and Commonwealth jurisdictions. This proposal was strongly resisted by countries that favoured the unitary approach to boards and was not pursued.

The 1980s saw the opening of financial markets around the

world. Hostile takeovers of companies reinforced the market for control in the Anglo-American economies. Many state enterprises were privatised. Greed became acceptable, if not respectable, and a glut of corporate scandals made a need for better board-level behaviour apparent. The phrase corporate governance appeared for the first time.

Codes of best practice in corporate governance were drafted, starting with Cadbury (1992) in the UK, followed by Hilmer (1993) in Australia, King (1995) in South Africa, Viénot (1995) in France and many more. The codes were not based on research showing relationships between governance standards and corporate performance or the protection of shareholders' interests; rather they reflected current ideas on best practice. Nevertheless, their introduction brought many changes to board behaviour around the world.

In most cases the codes were voluntary, relying on reporting and stock exchange listing rules for enforcement. Cadbury called for non-executive directors on the board, emphasised the importance of independence in these outside directors and argued for the separation of the roles of chief executive and chairman. It also proposed various board-level committees made up mainly of outside directors, including audit committees to provide a bridge between the external auditor and the board, remuneration committees to assess senior management rewards and nomination committees to suggest new candidates for the board. The idea was that the outside directors on these committees would bring an independent perspective to the deliberations and avoid domination by over-powerful executive directors.

The national codes were followed by such international codes as the OECD Code (1998) and the Commonwealth Code (1999). Institutional investors, such as CalPERS (the Californian State Employees Pension Fund), proposed codes for international companies looking for capital. Typically, they called for transparency and disclosure, the protection of minority shareholder interests and voting procedures which enabled shareholders to influence corporate decisions. The argument advanced by these (principally American) institutions is that if companies in other countries want to access their capital

markets, they must meet their governance standards. An indis-
putable argument? Not if you believe that if you want to invest
in another country's wealth and its companies' potential for
growth, profit and cash flow, you must accept the risks inherent
in those countries' governance practices.

The corporate governance debate

At the dawn of the 21st century, codes of best practice in corporate governance were in place in many countries and the importance of good corporate governance was widely recognised.
Directors were apparently – especially in the United States –
doing a good job in governing their companies. Indeed, there
was pressure for the international adoption of American legally
oriented approaches to corporate governance and generally accepted accounting principles (GAAP).

Then disaster struck. One of the largest companies in America,
Enron, an energy company, collapsed as a result of huge and un-
reported indebtedness. The failure of WorldCom, a telecommunications company, led to an even bigger bankruptcy. The
financial transparency, indeed the viability, of other companies
was questioned. Suddenly, instead of being seen as the innovative and responsible drivers of economic success, executive directors were viewed as greedy, short-sighted and more
interested in their personal share options than creating real and
sustainable shareholder value. This in turn led to the effectiveness of non-executive directors being questioned: in the case of
Enron and other companies, what were they doing while the
executive directors destroyed the company? Some blamed pressure from institutional investors, struggling to maintain the net
worth of their funds as stockmarkets fell; others blamed board
level attitudes and greed.

Governance problems appeared in companies in other parts
of the world, at Marconi and Tomkins in Britain, HIH Insurance
in Australia and Vodaphone Mannesmann in Germany, for
example. Andersen, one of the big five global accounting firms,
which was auditor of Enron, WorldCom and other firms with
dubious governance such as Waste Management, collapsed as
clients changed auditors and partners changed firms. The GAAP

were criticised for being based on rules that could be manipulated, rather than on the principles of overall fairness required in international accounting standards.

The Sarbanes-Oxley Act, placing new legal demands on directors of all companies listed in the United States, was rushed through. The New York Stock Exchange and NASDAQ changed their listing rules. Only independent directors can now serve on audit and remuneration committees, shareholders must approve directors' stock options and subsidised loans to directors are forbidden. Audit firms must rotate the audit partners dealing with individual clients, to prevent overfamiliarity. Auditors are forbidden to sell some non-audit services to audit clients, and audit staff must serve a cooling-off period before joining the staff of an audit client.

As has happened before, corporate collapses have led to changes to corporate governance thinking and practice. The agonising over governance processes has highlighted some important questions, which remain largely unanswered.

Should the CEO also be chairman of the board?

Most codes of corporate governance practice recommend that the roles of chairman of the board and CEO should be held by different people, thus providing checks and balances against domination of decision-making and over-enthusiastic risk-taking by an all-powerful individual.

The UK Combined Code does recognise that in some circumstances a single leader may be inevitable; in this case, it calls for a strong group of non-executives on the board with their own appointed leader. However, in the United States the roles of chairman and CEO are typically combined and held by a powerful individual, who leads the company in both managerial and governance matters. The question is which is preferable: a dominant leader who enhances performance; or shared responsibility, which reduces risk? This issue is sometimes called the duality question.

Can outside directors be genuinely independent?

A basic tenet in the corporate governance codes is the need for outside, non-executive directors who are independent of management. Independence, the literature argues, means having no interest in that company which might affect the exercise of objective judgment, other than their directorship and, perhaps, a small shareholding. So, for example, people who are contractually linked with the firm, are relations of the chairman or chief executive, or are retired executives of the firm, though they may have a contribution to make to board deliberations, would not be considered independent.

But can any director be genuinely independent, and be seen by the outside world to be independent, when their nomination to the board came from the members of that board, frequently from the CEO or chairman? Can directors really be independent when they work closely with the executive board members on strategic and other matters? How can independence be shown if they are personally involved in making decisions about issues that they are supposed to be monitoring? As one board chairman remarked, "The problem with many boards is that the directors are marking their own examination papers."

A different approach is adopted in continental Europe by separating outside and executive directors into two-tier boards, with no common membership. The upper supervisory board consists of outside directors, who monitor and control the work of the lower executive board, which run the enterprise. The independence question does not, therefore, arise. But proponents of the unitary board emphasise the value of having executive and non-executive directors working together, drawing on outside experience and perspective to identify key issues and formulate strategy. The more remote the outside directors are from the workings of the company, they argue, the less is the value of such board interaction.

Two recent proposals are that institutional investors should play an increased role in monitoring and influencing board decisions; and that shareholder representatives should elect another governance forum such as a corporate senate.

In the absence of a true separation of function between outside and executive directors, the answer is to appoint non-executives strong enough to be, and be seen to be, independent-minded. This is not easy.

Should institutional investors exercise more power?

Many commentators have called for institutional investors to "exercise their power" and vote the shares they hold on motions before company meetings. But despite these calls, many fund managers show little interest in the governance of companies in which they invest, preferring to "vote with their feet", trading their shares rather than incurring the costs of involvement in governance.

Moreover, the primary responsibility of institutional investors, such as investment trusts, mutual funds, unit trusts, life assurance companies or banks running portfolios for clients, is to their members. If they do vote their shares, it must be in the interests of those beneficial owners, whose objectives may well differ. A related issue, of importance when stockmarkets fall, is the accountability of institutional investors who get deeply involved in the governance of companies in which they have invested.

Are external auditors really independent?

The principal role of the external auditors is to report that the financial accounts, produced by the directors for the shareholders, truly reflect the state of the company's finances. Clearly, these auditors need to be independent of the company and its directors. However, as companies and firms of auditors have both become bigger, a problem has arisen.

The audit process involves a close and continuing relationship with the company and its executives. Consequently, the audit can provide a platform for the audit firm to offer non-audit work to its client, such as tax consulting, management consulting and information technology services. Many of the big global accounting firms were earning much more in non-audit work from some of their clients than the audit fee. Can the auditor then still be, and be seen to be, independent of the client?

Various proposals have been made to resolve the conflict or "overfamiliarity" issue: the periodic rotation of audit partners, a mandatory change of auditors every few years (strenuously resisted by the major audit firms), or the hiving off of non-audit work.

How should directors' remuneration be determined?

In the 1980s, the corporate governance *cri de coeur* was about directors protecting themselves from hostile takeovers by devices such as poison pills, greenmail and white knights.

More recently, concern has shifted to executive directors' remuneration. The senior managers of global corporations wield enormous power. Claiming to reflect owners' interests, directors are seen by some to be pursuing their own agendas and extracting huge rewards. Golden handshakes or handcuffs, rolling contracts, generous share options and other "incentive" packages have all contributed to them being called "fat cats". Most criticised, though, are those directors who have been rewarded handsomely when their company's performance has been dismal.

The preferred solution, in the corporate governance literature, is for a board remuneration committee, comprised entirely of outside directors, to determine executive directors' remuneration. The problem with this, as noted above, is whether such directors are genuinely independent or are really members of the "club". Other proposals for monitoring directors' rewards have included mandatory shareholder voting on directors' rewards or legislation that would impose statutory duties. Director remuneration consultancies, to advise on appropriate reward systems and levels, have blossomed. Overall, it is vital to be able to explain and justify directors' remuneration, particularly the rewards of the executive directors.

How should new complex, dynamic corporate entities be governed?

The original corporate concept did not envisage the complexity of today's organisational structures. In international business, these can involve complex networks of subsidiary and associated companies, companies with off-balance-sheet vehicles, chains of companies, giving leveraged power to companies at the top of the chain, limited partnerships controlling listed companies, groups with cross-holdings of shares and cross-directorships, and other networks with joint ventures and strategic alliances. Frequently, these networks of corporate interest operate in multiple jurisdictions, cultures and currencies. They may have voracious appetites for growth, with the attendant risks.

Such entities raise significant questions for corporate governance and financial reporting, as the employees, creditors and shareholders of Enron discovered. Moreover, these organisational forms can be dynamic and evolve rapidly. Corporate regulation and financial disclosure rules struggle to keep pace. Corporate governance processes have to respond, and directors must be sensitive to the implications of operating with complex, dynamic organisational and financial forms.

Is convergence taking place?

Securities regulation and corporate governance rules for the world's listed companies are converging. The International Organisation of Securities Commissions (IOSCO), to which the bulk of the world's securities regulatory bodies now belong, is a force behind the convergence of governance practices in listed companies. For example, its members have agreed to exchange information on unusual trades, thus making global insider trading more hazardous for those that engage in it. The International Accounting Standards Committee (IASC) and the International Auditing Practices Committee (IPAC) have close links with IOSCO and are both working towards international harmonisation and standardisation of financial reporting and auditing practices.

The need to raise capital internationally is also driving governance practices towards internationally accepted norms. The efforts of international bodies, such as the World Bank, the Commonwealth and the OECD, in recommending codes of good corporate governance, have also encouraged convergence.

However, there are forces that can be said to discourage convergence. Company, contract and competition law differ between jurisdictions, and so do the powers and reliability of the courts. Market capitalisation, ownership patterns and the liquidity of stockmarkets vary, as do the listing rules of stock exchanges. Board structures and governance practices can be very different, often reflecting the history and culture of specific countries and ethnic groupings – for example, the experience of corporate governance in Japan, the two-tier board structures and worker co-determination found in continental European countries and the family domination, even in listed companies, of the overseas Chinese in countries throughout East Asia.

What makes for a good director and a better board?

Some people expect board-level discussions to be rational, based on rigorous reviews of alternatives. In reality, board meetings involve a political process. The position and prestige of board members do not guarantee a successful board: the chairman of Enron's audit committee was a leading accounting academic.

Corporate governance is more about human behaviour than about structures, strictures, rules or regulations. The calibre and styles of directors largely determine the effectiveness of the board. Board interactions can involve intrigue, secrecy and conspiracy, as well as relationships based on honesty, fairness and trust. After recent high profile corporate collapses, many felt that directors had been putting their own interests before those of anyone else – often shamelessly and sometimes with disregard for the law. In doing so they had undermined the trust placed in them and harmed the well-being of investors, employees and communities.

The three overriding attributes of a good director are integrity, competence and knowledge. Integrity is fundamental. Directors look after the shareholders' interests. They have a fiduciary duty to the company to act openly and honestly for the good of all members. Although they may be significant shareholders, the enterprise does not belong to them personally. Any potential conflict of interest must be made clear as soon as possible. Any personal gain a director makes from the company's activities must be open and (to use an apt phrase) completely above board.

Directors need specific core competencies, such as strategic vision, reasoning and planning capabilities, a decision-making ability, communication skills, political awareness and networking know-how. A well-constructed board will have a comprehensive range of such competencies among its members. Directors must have minds of their own and be able to work as part of a team. Understanding the organisation itself is vital, as is knowledge about the business it is in. See the core competencies of directors in Appendix 3. Director training and updating are crucial in today's changing governance climate.

However, because every corporate entity is different, directors' contributions vary. They bring different knowledge, skills and experiences to their board. But all directors need an essential body of knowledge about the enterprise if they are to make sense of board information and contribute meaningfully to board discussion. This knowledge has three parts.

1 Knowledge of the corporate entity includes a clear understanding of the basis of power (who the members of the organisation are and where the power lies to appoint the governing body); the basis of law under which the body operates and what the governance rules and regulations are (for a limited company, these are company law and the company's memorandum and articles of association); the board structure, membership and personalities; and the board processes, such as the use of board committees and the basis of board information. An awareness of the history of the entity is also important in interpreting the current situation and understanding the board culture and the perspectives of other board members.

2 Knowledge of the business embraces an understanding of the basic business processes, its purpose and aims, its strengths and weaknesses and how it measures success, its field of operations (including markets, competitors and its current operating context), the strategies being pursued, the structure of the organisation, its culture, management and people, and the form of management control and management control systems. Risk assessment is an important role of a governing body.

3 Knowledge of the financials includes an awareness of how the company is financed, a sound understanding of its annual accounts, accounting principles and directors' reports, together with an awareness of developing trends in key financial ratios, the criteria used in investment appraisals, the calibre of financial controls and who the auditors are. It is not necessary to be an accountant to be a good director; indeed, some would argue the reverse. But it is crucial to be able to appreciate the financial aspects of the company.

It is said that "outside directors never know enough about the business to be useful and inside directors always know too much to be independent". An effective board will be made up of committed, independent, tough-minded executive and non-executive directors who work together with trust and mutual understanding.

By contrast, poorly performing directors may lack sufficient time or commitment. They may have insufficient interest or, worse, be motivated by self-interest. Complacency, arrogance and the need to dominate are all board-level failings, as are being weak-willed and easily led. "Yes men" who fail to speak out when they strongly disagree are as dishonest as those who deliberately lie.

A newly appointed director needs a proper induction programme, to reduce the learning time taken before beginning to make a significant contribution to the board. The quicker a new director masters this knowledge, the faster and the better is the contribution to board deliberations. See the induction checklist for directors in Appendix 4.

Sound boards have sound leadership. The role of the chairman of the board is crucial. Meetings are not just held; they have to be planned, managed and led. Board members need relevant and timely information. Some may need additional briefing. In badly led boards, personalities and politics prevail.

There are growing calls for the monitoring of board performance. Despite the existence of rigorous appraisal systems for managers, most boards do not attempt to evaluate the contribution of individual directors or assess the overall performance of the board. At best, the chairman makes an informal assessment. Some directors argue that the published performance of the company is enough. But, increasingly, institutional shareholders and others are making demands for more competent chairmen, better directors and improved board performance. Moreover, approaches are being pioneered to monitor directors and board performance (see the checklist on board effectiveness in Appendix 5). It can only be a matter of time before these become required and the results published.

Ultimately, corporate governance is about the way power is exercised over corporate entities. The issue is who wields that power and what are the attitudes of the powerful. Power may be derived in many ways: from the legal standing of the board, from a dominant or charismatic leader, through pressure from significant shareholders, the influence of the auditors, the ambitions of financial markets, the threat of litigation, the effects of legislation and regulation, changing public expectations and external exhortation, even the recommendations of international organisations. Today any of them could present directors with a significant challenge. There is not one right way to govern corporations, but there are many wrong ones.

The 19th century saw the foundations laid for modern corporations; it was the century of the entrepreneur. The 20th century became the century of management. Now the 21st century promises to be the century of governance, as the focus swings towards the legitimacy and the effectiveness of directors and boards around the world and the way power is exercised over corporate entities. The field of corporate governance is expanding and changing quickly. Directors and prospective directors need all the help they can get in meeting the challenges.

A to Z

A and B shares

Normally, each share in a company carries one vote. Indeed, "one share, one vote" is a basic tenet of SHAREHOLDER DEMOCRACY. But some companies do create different classes of shares. One reason is to give a class of share different terms, such as preferential rights on winding up or prior claims on profits. On the opening of the Chinese stockmarkets, "A" shares were available only to Chinese citizens resident in China; "B" shares were available to foreigners. This differentiation has subsequently been relaxed. Another reason is to increase capital, while keeping control in the hands of a few dominant shareholders. Thus a class of share is issued, typically referred to as a "B" share, which carries a disproportionate number of votes per share. For years the famous Savoy/Claridges Hotel group protected itself with a second tier of shares carrying 20 times the VOTING RIGHTS of the shares listed on the stockmarket. The company was finally sold to American investors in 1998. (See CHINESE CORPORATE GOVERNANCE and DUAL VOTING RIGHTS.)

ABI

See ASSOCIATION OF BRITISH INSURERS.

Accountability

The directors of a company are primarily accountable to their SHAREHOLDERS. Such accountability is normally achieved through the regular DIRECTORS' REPORT AND ACCOUNTS and the ANNUAL GENERAL MEETING of the shareholder members of the company. In many jurisdictions, however, there have been calls for wider accountability from boards, particularly in PUBLIC COMPANIES. REGULATORS demand wider DISCLOSURE of financial and other information. Employees' representatives expect information on matters that could affect their interests. (In Germany, the Netherlands and Sweden employees

A have statutory rights to board-level accountability.) Customer and other interest groups call for greater transparency of company activities. STAKEHOLDER THEORY argues that public companies have a duty to be accountable to all interest groups that could be affected by the company's actions (including customers, distributors, employees, financial institutions and suppliers, as well as local, national and international public interests).

The directors of companies, being managers rather of other people's money than their own, it cannot well be expected that they should watch over it with the same anxious vigilance with which the partners in a private copartnery (business) frequently watch over their own.

Adam Smith, *Wealth of Nations*, 1776

Accountancy Foundation

The REGULATOR of the UK accounting industry, launched in 2002. Funded by the six UK accountancy professional bodies, the foundation operates through a Review Board, which delegates responsibilities to the Auditing Practices Board, the Ethics Standards Board and the Investigation and Disciplinary Board. Delays and difficulties arose from the outset. Despite claims that the UK has an almost infallible regulatory structure, complaints of overcomplexity, duplication and unclear boundaries were heard. Some urged the government to have the self-regulatory regime taken over by the FINANCIAL REPORTING COUNCIL. (Compare with the American regulator, the PUBLIC ACCOUNTABILITY BOARD.)

Accounting Oversight Board

See PUBLIC COMPANY ACCOUNTING OVERSIGHT BOARD.

Accounting Standards Board

A

A UK body which makes, amends and withdraws accounting standards. (See also FINANCIAL REPORTING COUNCIL.)

Added-value chain

Industries and individual businesses must add value to their products or services to satisfy their customers. In the food industry, for example, the farmer grows wheat, the flour mills turn it into flour, the transport company carries it to the baker where it is baked, or to the supermarket, where it is sold to the end user. Each link in the chain adds value. The flour mills add value to the grain by the various milling and packaging processes. The supermarket adds value by buying in bulk, displaying and providing customer service. A business may be heavily integrated along the value-added chain or it may outsource all but a CORE COMPETENCE. Reebok, a shoe firm, has few manufacturing and no retailing outlets, only a highly profitable managerial and marketing function. Analysing the elements of the added-value chain in a business can provide some valuable strategic insights. Figure 5 illustrates a value-chain analysis for an electricity supplier.

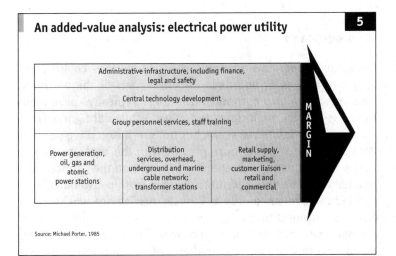

An added-value analysis: electrical power utility   **5**

Administrative infrastructure, including finance, legal and safety			M A R G I N
Central technology development			
Group personnel services, staff training			
Power generation, oil, gas and atomic power stations	Distribution services, overhead, underground and marine cable network; transformer stations	Retail supply, marketing, customer liaison – retail and commercial	

Source: Michael Porter, 1985

A   Each of the boxes in Figure 5 can, obviously, be expanded into a whole set or hierarchy of more detailed diagrams that show where value is being added in the company's processes. If associated with the related costs, a value-chain analysis can highlight which elements of the processes are driving costs and which are adding value. This information can be important in STRATEGY FORMULATION, because it can pinpoint what gives the business its strategic advantage and how its activities are differentiated from those of competitors. It can suggest new strategic options, both for improving existing activities and for developing new strategies such as outsourcing, growth by ac-quisition or mergers, STRATEGIC ALLIANCES to obtain scale economies, share risk or enhance development.

Adjournment of meetings

See MEETING MANIPULATION.

ADR

See AMERICAN DEPOSITARY RECEIPT.

Advisory boards

Companies operating internationally sometimes create advi-sory committees or boards in different parts of the world, to give advice to the corporate directors. Typically, prominent business leaders, politicians and other influential figures from the region are invited to serve, but not given executive powers. Advisory boards were more prevalent in the 1970s and early 1980s. Subsequently, companies found that the advice they needed could be obtained more cheaply from consultants, who needed to be retained only as long as their advice was wanted. Some also found that advisory boards, although they had no formal executive authority, assumed an independence that created complications by making policy recommendations

which were inconsistent with group-wide needs. An advisory
board might, for example, call for investment in a given
country, when the board's global strategy called for disinvest-
ment there.

Age of directors

Three factors restrict the age of directors: company law, which
typically requires directors to be under 70 unless the SHARE-
HOLDERS have duly approved an exception; the company's
own ARTICLES OF ASSOCIATION; and, for LISTED COMPA-
NIES, the LISTING RULES of the relevant stock exchange.
OUTSIDE DIRECTORS are generally older than EXECUTIVE DI-
RECTORS.

*Once on the board, directors seem to stay for ever. I would like to see a
"sell-by" date stamped on the head of every director.*
David Norburn, 1993

Agency theory

A statistically powerful, theoretical approach to CORPORATE
GOVERNANCE. As Michael Jensen and William Meckling, the
proponents of agency theory, explained in an article in the
Journal of Financial Economics in 1976:

> *Agency theory involves a contract under which one or more persons
> (the shareholders) engage another person (the directors) to perform
> some service on their behalf which includes delegating some decision-
> making authority to the agent. If both parties to the relationship are
> utility maximisers there is good reason to believe the agent will not
> always act in the best interests of the principal.*

In other words, directors pursue their own interests and
cannot be trusted to act in the interests of the SHAREHOLDERS.
Checks and balances mechanisms are needed. There is ample
anecdotal evidence to support this contention: directors who

A treat listed, PUBLIC COMPANIES as though they are their own property, like Al (Chainsaw) Dunlap of SUNBEAM; or who dominate their boards, like Robert MAXWELL; or who fail to act in the interests of their shareholders, like Bernie Ebbers of WORLDCOM. A lot of research on board-level activities has been published using agency-theory methods. Much of this work has been based on aggregated, published data, and has been done by young researchers who have never met a company director. In the field of financial economics, agency theory offers a statistically rigorous insight into corporate governance processes. Reality, unfortunately, is often more complicated. Board behaviour does not consist of sets of con-tractual relationships, but is influenced by interpersonal be-haviour, group dynamics and political intrigue. Nor do all directors act in a way that maximises their own personal inter-ests; they can act responsibly with independence and integrity, as envisaged by the alternative STEWARDSHIP THEORY. Never-theless, insights from agency research have challenged the shib-boleths of conventional wisdom about the way boards work.

Statistical methods will not explain the reality of the boardroom.
Ada Demb, 1993

No man, acting as agent, can be allowed to put himself into a position in which his interest and his duty will be in conflict.
Lord Cairns, giving judgment in the London High Court in 1874

Agenda

The programme of business to be covered in a meeting. Three approaches to agenda design can be distinguished.

1 The routine approach, in which each meeting follows the pattern of the previous one (apologies, approval of the MINUTES, matters arising, the usual substantive items and any other business).
2 The CHAIRMAN-led approach, in which the chairman deter-mines the agenda. Sir Norman Chester, who became Warden of

Nuffield College, Oxford, after a career in Whitehall, believed **A** that a good chairman, among whom he counted himself, should put much effort into designing agenda. Care should be taken in choosing the items to be discussed, allocating time to each item and positioning each item on the agenda. Matters likely to be controversial should come towards the end, he recommended, when members were expecting the meeting to end, or had already left, thus increasing the chairman's chances of getting the decision he wants. He also believed in drafting the minutes along with the agenda, because a sound chairman always has a preferred outcome. He knew that those who draft the minutes wield the power.

3 The professional chairman approach, in which the chairman seeks advice on the agenda, perhaps from the COMPANY SEC-RETARY, or as some chairmen do by asking each director whether there are items they wish to have discussed. Lord Caldecote, when chairman of the Delta Group, wrote to each of his directors periodically to ask whether there were matters they felt that the board should be discussing for the future benefit of the firm.

Which approach is adopted depends on the BOARD STYLE.

Life is a constant struggle between honour and inclination.
Anon

AGM

See ANNUAL GENERAL MEETING.

AIMA

Short for the Australian Investment Managers Association, a fre-quent source of SHAREHOLDER ACTIVISM in Australia. The AIMA advises its clients on issues and recommends PROXY VOTING actions. (See also ABA, NAPF and PIRC.)

A Alliance

See GAMES DIRECTORS PLAY.

Alternate director

The ARTICLES OF ASSOCIATION of some companies allow the board to nominate alternates for directors. This can be useful if board members have to travel a lot or are based out of the country in which BOARD MEETINGS are usually held. When serving in the alternate capacity, the alternate director has all the rights to INFORMATION and all the duties and responsibilities of a normal director.

Annual general meeting

A properly convened meeting of the voting SHAREHOLDERS of a company. The annual general meeting (AGM) is part of the formal machinery of CORPORATE GOVERNANCE, requiring the directors to demonstrate their ACCOUNTABILITY to the owners. Certain decisions, such as the approval of the annual accounts and dividend, the appointment of directors and the confirmation of the AUDITORS are statutorily required to be taken by the AGM. The detailed rules, such as the amount of notice required and for voting (including proxy votes), are usually contained in the company's ARTICLES OF ASSOCIATION. Some jurisdictions allow small, CLOSELY HELD COMPANIES to forgo their AGM, because all members can be presumed to know and be able to influence the company's affairs. In the United States, and increasingly in the UK, directors of LISTED COMPANIES expect to be extensively questioned at their AGMS. Indeed, they are often briefed, even rehearsed, on possible enquiries. INSTITUTIONAL INVESTORS as well as private investors now demand answers to questions on matters such as DIRECTORS' REMUNERATION and the company's (and by implication its board's) performance. Otherwise AGMS are generally brief, formal, entirely predictable

occasions in which any sign of critical questioning is thwarted
from the chair and the only shareholder comment is a vote of
thanks to the chairman and the board. Recently, however,
there have been signs of an end to that complacency. In Japan,
the AGMS of nearly all listed companies are held on the same
day to prevent the disruption of the meeting by paid trouble-
makers from the YAKUSA.

Amakaduri

See DESCENT FROM HEAVEN.

American Depositary Receipt

The vehicle for a foreign company to be listed on an American
stock exchange. An American depositary receipt (ADR) is a security issued, for a fee, by an American investment bank that
holds a matching number of real shares in the company. (See
also GLOBAL SHARES.)

*If, in the 1990s, Arthur Andersen had been less envious of the high-
rolling consultants at its former twin, now called Accenture, and had not
gone chasing blindly after business, it might now have a future.*
The Economist, July 27th 2002

ANDERSEN

Previously known as Arthur Andersen, one of the world's top
five accounting firms, which collapsed following a number of
audit failures, including WASTE MANAGEMENT, WORLDCOM
and ENRON. This damaged the confidence of the entire accounting profession, which suddenly realised that the market,
not professional self-regulation, was in control. Memorably,
ENRON shredded papers sought by an SEC investigation, and
appeared before a grand jury on charges of obstructing justice.
Clients quickly distanced themselves and Andersen partners

A

around the world smartly joined one of the remaining BIG FOUR global audit firms.

Articles of association

The formal set of rules by which a company is run. Registered with the company regulatory authorities at the time of incorporation, in accordance with the company law in that jurisdiction, the articles provide an important element in CORPORATE GOVERNANCE mechanisms. Articles can be amended by a resolution formally approved by a meeting of the company's members. Directors should always study the articles of a company on whose board they serve. Occasionally, non-standard drafting can have unexpected effects on director powers and board decisions. For example, an owner-manager of a company incorporated in the UK, which was in a JOINT VENTURE with a Japanese SHAREHOLDER, was thwarted in his attempt to bring in new capital. He believed he had control because he held 61% of the voting shares, only to discover that to exercise such powers, the articles required the approval of 75% of the shareholders.

Asian values

One of the explanations offered to explain decades of economic success throughout East Asia: business and governance practices rooted in a strong work ethic, a commitment to saving and a family-centred culture. Following the financial and economic collapses of countries such as Indonesia, Malaysia, Thailand and South Korea in 1997/98, CRONY CAPITALISM was offered as an alternative insight.

Associate director

Some companies give the title of director to senior managers, even though they are not formally members of the board. The reason may be to reward managerial performance with recognition and status, or to give prestige to an executive who is required to represent the company with clients, customers or government. Sometimes such employees are called associate directors. Even though they have not been appointed by the SHAREHOLDERS, or recognised as directors by the filing requirements of companies' acts and stock exchange listing agreements, such people could find themselves held responsible like other directors if those with whom they had dealt reasonably thought they were directors. (See TITLES OF DIRECTORS.)

Association of British Insurers

An organisation representing the interests of INSTITUTIONAL INVESTORS among British insurance companies, which has taken a higher profile in CORPORATE GOVERNANCE issues in recent years, monitoring company activities against codes of good corporate governance conduct, occasionally advising on SHAREHOLDER ACTIVISM and PROXY VOTING options. The Association of British Insurers (ABI) has issued guidelines on the INFORMATION its members would like to receive from companies in which they invest. (See also NATIONAL ASSOCIATION OF PENSION FUNDS.)

www.abi.org.uk

Audit

In most jurisdictions companies are required to have an audit by external, independent AUDITORS, who report to the SHAREHOLDERS that the annual report and accounts presented to them by the directors show a true and fair view of the state of the company's affairs. Although the exact wording varies by jurisdiction, the intention is to provide an independent verification of the directors' financial report. In some places, quarterly accounts also have to be audited; in others, private CLOSELY HELD COMPANIES may dispense with the audit, if

A the shareholders agree; and in a few, such as the British Virgin Islands, there is no audit requirement at all.

Audit committee

A subcommittee of the main board, whose responsibilities and visibility have increased over the years. Initially, the audit committee's role was to act as a bridge between the external AUDITORS and the board. Powerful EXECUTIVE DIRECTORS, such as the finance director and the CEO, could become too close to the external auditors, resolving issues before they reached the board. Typically, an audit committee would meet three or four times a year to discuss the details of the audit, to consider any contentious points that had arisen on the accounts and to receive the auditor's recommendations on AUDIT-related matters such as management controls. The audit committee often negotiated the audit fee.

Audit committees will fall short of their potential if they lack the understanding to deal adequately with the auditing or accounting matters that they are likely to face.
Cadbury Report, 1992

Following the failure of major companies such as ENRON, MARCONI and WORLDCOM, the need for greater control over senior executives has broadened the role of the audit committee. In a report published in 2003 for the UK's FINANCIAL REPORTING COUNCIL, Sir Robert Smith called for audit committees to monitor the integrity of their company's financial statements and review significant financial decisions. The committee should also be responsible for confirming the auditor's independence and effectiveness. Moreover, audit committees should comprise three independent NON-EXECUTIVE DIRECTORS, with at least one having recent and relevant financial experience. The audit committee CHAIRMAN must be available to answer questions at the AGM. Companies not meeting these requirements must explain why not in their annual reports.

All the CODES OF BEST PRACTICE in CORPORATE GOVERN-

ANCE call for audit committees. The New York Stock Exchange requires one, composed entirely of independent OUTSIDE DIRECTORS, as a condition of listing. Following the Enron and WorldCom failures, there have been calls in the United States for the role of audit committees to be enhanced, making them responsible for the appointment of the auditors and for fulfilling other executive oversight and corporate governance functions. However, some see this as a move towards a European-style TWO-TIER BOARD; others fear that such an audit committee would interfere in management's legitimate responsibilities. (See also NEW YORK STOCK EXCHANGE LISTING RULES and RISK MANAGEMENT.)

If something serious is going on, the audit committee will have to pursue it to the end, even if it becomes adversarial.
Sir Robert Smith, chairman, Weir Group

Experience has shown that audit committees have developed into essential committees of boards of directors.
European Commission Report, 1996 Green Paper on Auditing

The central issue is that audit committees are comprised of good-quality non-executive directors with the right mix of skills who can be trusted to make the right decisions.
Rodger Hughes, PricewaterhouseCoopers

Auditors

The independent, outside auditors fulfil a crucial role in CORPORATE GOVERNANCE. Usually appointed formally by the SHAREHOLDERS, on the recommendation of the incumbent board, the auditors report on the truth and fairness of the financial accounts. Should the AUDIT throw up disagreements which cannot be reconciled with the company's directors, the auditor will qualify the audit report. In recent years, auditors of major PUBLIC COMPANIES around the world have found themselves the subject of LITIGATION from dissatisfied shareholders, challenging the validity of the audited accounts. Sometimes this is

A because the company has failed and the auditors, who are insured, are a last resort, the so-called DEEP POCKET SYNDROME. Following ENRON's and other corporate collapses, the independence of some auditors has been questioned, particularly when they generate more money from consulting work with the client than from the audit fee. So has the practice of accountants, who have been involved in the audit, leaving the audit firm and joining the finance staff of the client. The European Union has recommended that partners involved in performing audits should not join the audit client before the end of a two-year cooling-off period. Guidelines from the Institute of Chartered Accountants in England and Wales require an assessment of threats to independence through self-interest, self-review, advocacy, familiarity or intimidation. They also call for the partner responsible for an audit to be rotated periodically, to avoid the danger of overfamiliarity with the client. The audit partner of MAXWELL never changed.

Auditors owe external loyalty, consultants internal.
Allen Sykes, *Capitalism for Tomorrow*, 2002

Auditors are like the cuckoos in cuckoo clocks: they come out, comment briefly and nip back inside. Ticking is what they do best.
Robert Hodgkinson, chairman, Financial Reporting Council, London

---

Aufsichtsrat

The upper SUPERVISORY BOARD of the German TWO-TIER BOARD (see GERMAN CORPORATE GOVERNANCE).

B share

See A AND B SHARES and DUAL VOTING RIGHTS.

Backdoor listing

See SHELL COMPANY.

Big four

The four global accounting firms which AUDIT the majority of global corporations. There were more, but following mergers and the collapse of ANDERSEN, only four major firms – Deloitte Touche, Ernst & Young, KPMG, PricewaterhouseCoopers – now remain. Various government and regulatory bodies have been reviewing the implications for competition policy. In 2002, AUDIT fees for the UK's FTSE 100 companies represented about a quarter of the total fees paid by them to the big four. In both the UK and the United States the proportion of non-audit work is slowly reducing.

Board assessment

Management assessment is a routine practice in most large companies. Yet the most significant organ of the company, the board, is seldom assessed. In 1998, the HAMPEL REPORT called for formal procedures to "assess both the board's collective performance and that of individual directors". But research three years later by PricewaterhouseCoopers showed that only one-third of UK companies had done so. The Conference Board's Corporate Governance Research Centre published *Determining Board Effectiveness* (1999), which offered a set of questions that go to the heart of board assessment.

- How does the board define its role and duties?
- How does the board prioritise its responsibilities?

B

- How effectively does the board monitor company performance?
- Does the board have sufficient independence to perform its duties properly?
- Does the board have the right mix of skills to achieve its goals?
- Does the board have the right size and structure?
- How does the board oversee auditing functions to minimise risk?
- How does the board best structure and use its nominating committee?
- What is the board's role in determining director and executive compensation?
- How does the board conduct CEO appointment and succession planning?
- Are the board's decision-making processes effective?
- Does the board have a process for evaluating whether it is achieving its goals?
- Can the board make course corrections if necessary?
- Does the board communicate effectively to investors?

(See also BOARD DEVELOPMENT.)

www.boardroomanalysis.com, www.corpmon.com

It is a useful though often painful exercise for a board to ask: How did we do? What lessons can be learned? How can we do better?

Daniel Hodson, Gresham College, London

Board corporate governance policies

The increasing focus on corporate governance has caused some boards to articulate their CORPORATE GOVERNANCE policies, and in some cases to publish them. General Motors, for example, has extensive guidelines for the board. These include guidance on:

- the separation of CHAIRMAN and CEO;
- the concept of a LEAD DIRECTOR overseeing specific functions and areas of the business;

- board committees;
- the assignment and rotation of committee members;
- the frequency and length of committee meetings;
- committee AGENDA;
- the selection of agenda items for BOARD MEETINGS;
- board materials to be distributed in advance;
- presentations to the directors;
- regular attendance of non-directors at board meetings;
- executive sessions of OUTSIDE DIRECTORS;
- board access to senior management;
- board compensation review;
- size of the board;
- mix of inside and outside directors;
- definition of independence for outside directors;
- board membership of former CEOS;
- board membership criteria;
- selection of new directors;
- assessing the board's performance;
- directors who change their present job responsibilities;
- term limits and retirement age;
- evaluation of the CEO;
- board succession planning;
- top management development;
- board interaction with INSTITUTIONAL INVESTORS, the press, customers and other STAKEHOLDERS.

Other companies have followed suit with their own guidelines and policies on corporate governance.

The most important factor governing a successful board is the quality of the board itself ... Board meetings must not be solemn affairs ... There is no absolute magic formula. Every company has its own culture and metabolism, and different types of business require separate types of management style and approach from the board.
Sir Richard Greenbury

Board development

B Businesses have a tendency to outgrow their boards. A successful board in the past does not guarantee continuing success in the future. As the strategic circumstances facing a company change, new thinking and, perhaps, new faces are needed. Yet few boards have plans for director succession and development. Even fewer have a strategy for board development to ensure that the board evolves in line with proposed changes in the overall corporate strategy.

Board meeting

Boards of directors can meet when and where they want, subject to anything in the ARTICLES OF ASSOCIATION. Some boards have few meetings, either because the directors meet regularly on an informal basis, so that the board meetings become an occasion for formalising decisions taken, or because the activities of the company do not require more meetings. Professional boards, however, usually have a regular schedule of meetings (often monthly). (See also BOARD STYLE.)

> It is impossible to conceive of the corporation's (General Motors) board of directors having intimate knowledge of, and business experience, in every one of the technical matters which require top level consideration or action. Nevertheless the board can and should be responsible for the end result.
> Alfred P. Sloan, *My Years with General Motors*, 1963

Board performance

Board performance is under the spotlight as never before. SHAREHOLDERS, particularly INSTITUTIONAL SHAREHOLDERS, have much higher expectations of the boards of companies in which they invest than in the past. Boards need to establish criteria for their own performance, monitor their achievements and take remedial action when necessary. (See also COMMONWEALTH PRINCIPLES FOR CORPORATE GOVERNANCE, NEW YORK STOCK EXCHANGE LISTING RULES and Appendix 1.)

B

Coote got me in as a director of something or other. Very good business for me – nothing to do except go down into the City once or twice a year to one of those hotel places and sit around a table where they have some nice new blotting paper. Then Coote or some clever Johnny makes a speech simply bristling with figures, but fortunately you needn't listen to it – and I can tell you, you often get a jolly good lunch out of it.
Agatha Christie, *The Seven Dials*

Board structures

At its simplest, board structure distinguishes between those directors who hold management positions in the company and those who do not. Those with management positions are often referred to as EXECUTIVE DIRECTORS and those who do not as NON-EXECUTIVE DIRECTORS or OUTSIDE DIRECTORS. A further distinction can be drawn between those non-executive directors who are genuinely independent of the company (other than their directorship and, perhaps, a non-significant shareholding) and those who, though not employees, are in positions that might affect their independence and objectivity. (See INDEPENDENT DIRECTOR.)

Figure 1 on page 3 distinguishes management from governance by representing the GOVERNING BODY as a circle superimposed on the management triangle. This model can be applied to other board structures.

First there is the board made up entirely of executive directors (Figure 6 on the next page). In such boards, every director is also a managerial employee of the company. Many start-up and family firms have this structure, with the founder, close colleagues and other family members all working in the business and being members of the board. The boards of some subsidiary companies operating in groups also choose the all-executive board, which is, in effect, the senior management team of the business with no outside members. The boards of

B

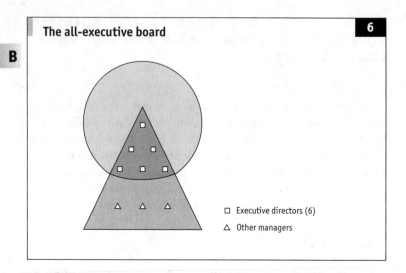

The all-executive board   6

□ Executive directors (6)
△ Other managers

major Japanese companies are typically large and effectively comprise executives from the company. (See JAPANESE CORPORATE GOVERNANCE.)

> *Q. What is your ideal board? A. My chief executive and myself.*
> Sir Terence Conran, chairman, Habitat, 2001

A potential problem of a board that is dominated by its executive directors is that they are, in effect, monitoring and supervising their own performance. One solution, other than appointing independent non-executive directors, is for the CHAIRMAN to discuss with newly appointed executive directors what is expected of them. Executive directors have to wear two hats, one as the manager of a part of the business, the other as a director responsible for the governance of the company. The important thing is not to be wearing the manager's hat in the boardroom.

Then there is the board with a majority of executive directors (Figure 7). In the evolution of companies and their boards, non-executive directors are appointed to boards for various reasons. Sometimes, in a developing PRIVATE COMPANY, the executive directors feel the need for additional expertise, knowledge or skills to supplement their own. Non-executive directors can also

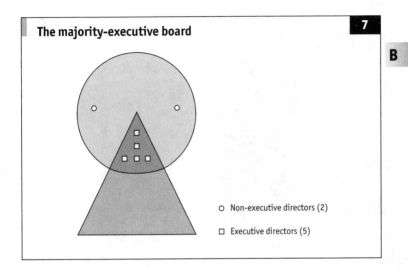

The majority-executive board   7

○ Non-executive directors (2)

□ Executive directors (5)

be appointed to be nominees for those investing equity or debt in the business, or to secure relationships with suppliers, customers or others in the added-value chain of the business. Another reason can be succession in a family firm, when shareholdings are split between branches of the family.

The practice of leading PUBLIC COMPANIES in Australia, the United States and increasingly in the UK is to have boards with

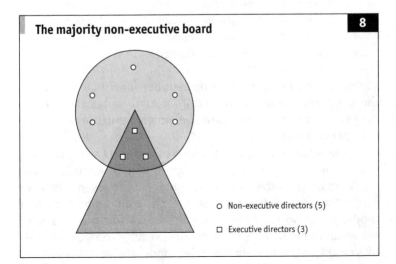

The majority non-executive board   8

○ Non-executive directors (5)

□ Executive directors (3)

B

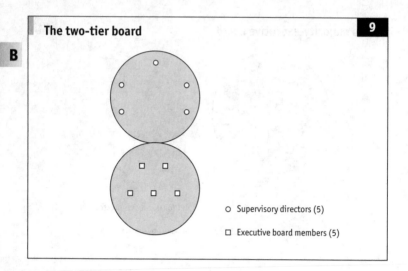

The two-tier board 9

○ Supervisory directors (5)

□ Executive board members (5)

a majority of non-executive directors. Indeed, in American LISTED COMPANIES the outside directors usually heavily outnumber the inside executive directors (Figure 8 on page 41).

> *What matters is not only the structure of boards but how they work.*
> Sir Adrian Cadbury, 1993

> *Corporate performance depends upon what boards do and how their members behave, not upon whether they have a particular committee structure.*
> Colin Coulson-Thomas, 2002

Some argue that if the outside members dominate the board, the governance process has really ceased to be a UNITARY BOARD but has moved towards the power structure of a TWO-TIER BOARD (Figure 9).

In the Anglo-American traditions of CORPORATE GOVERNANCE, the unitary board is the norm; that is, a single board made up of executive and non-executive directors in whatever proportion is thought appropriate. In the continental European model of corporate governance there is a two-tier board, in which an upper board supervises the executive board on behalf of STAKEHOLDERS. In the two-tier model the members of the

SUPERVISORY BOARD are totally separate from the senior management team. (See GERMAN CORPORATE GOVERNANCE.)

B

> *Fans of the existing mixed-up board can be reassured that no scheme relying on non-executive directors being tough-minded, hard-headed and independent has ever succeeded.*
> Shann Turnbull, 2002

Board styles

The CHAIRMAN of the board inevitably has an effect on the way that the board goes about its business. Board styles vary enormously. Figure 10 shows some of these, depending on the extent of the directors' concern for their interpersonal relationships at board level, on the one hand, and their tough-minded concern for the work of the board, on the other.

◪ **The rubber-stamp board** shows little concern either for the tasks of the board or the interpersonal relationships among the directors. Examples of such boards can be found in the "letter-box" companies registered in many offshore tax havens. The meetings of the board are a

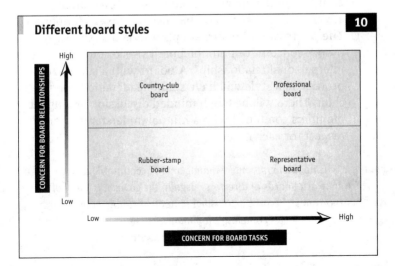

Different board styles   **10**

CONCERN FOR BOARD RELATIONSHIPS — High / Low

Country-club board

Professional board

Rubber-stamp board

Representative board

Low — CONCERN FOR BOARD TASKS — High

B

formality. Indeed, they are often minuted without them actually taking place. The boards of some private CLOSELY HELD COMPANIES also treat their BOARD MEETINGS as a formality; perhaps because one individual is dominant and takes the decisions, or because the key players see each other frequently and decisions are taken in the management context.

- **The country-club board**, in contrast, is very concerned with interpersonal relations at board level and the issues before the board may take second place. The boards of some old-established companies, which have been successful in the past, fit this model. There is likely to be a great deal of ritual about board meetings. The boardroom will be beautifully furnished, complete with sepia pictures of previous chairmen. Legends and myths surround board affairs. Meetings always follow the same pattern. Following the long-established traditions is revered. Innovation is discouraged.

- **The REPRESENTATIVE BOARD** places more emphasis on the tasks of the board than it does on board relations. Frequently, this type of board has directors representing different SHAREHOLDERS or STAKEHOLDERS. The board is more like a parliament of diverse interests. Issues can easily become politicised. Board discussions can be adversarial. The basis and balance of power is important.

- **The professional board** adopts a style that shows a proper concern for both the board's tasks and its interpersonal relationships. A board with a successful professional style will have sound leadership from the chair. There will be tough-minded discussion among the members combined with a mutual understanding and respect for each other.

...there was no attempt to make management accountable to anyone. On the contrary boards of directors – legally the governing body of the corporation – became increasingly impotent rubber stamps for a company's top management.
Peter Drucker, *Post-Capitalist Society*, 1993

*Boards should pay greater attention to the calibre as well as
the mix of directors, recognising that effective board membership
requires high levels of intellectual ability, experience,
soundness of judgement and integrity.*
Hilmer Report, *Strictly Boardroom*, 1993

*Until the 1990s the executives dominated boards in both the US and the
UK. Non-executives were mainly compliant cheerleaders.*
The Economist, November 2nd 2002

BRT

See BUSINESS ROUNDTABLE.

*Boards have an unlimited capacity for self-delusion.
The way they work is a black box.*
Andrew Pettigrew, 1997

Bullock Report

When Sir Alan Bullock (now Lord Bullock) was master of St
Catherine's College, Oxford, in 1976, he was asked to chair an
inquiry into industrial democracy by Harold Wilson, then prime
minister and leader of the Labour Party. This was a response to
the European Community's proposals, in the fifth draft directive on company law harmonisation, that major companies in
all EC countries should adopt the German TWO-TIER BOARD
structure, in which one half of the members of the SUPERVI-
SORY BOARD represented capital (elected by the shareholders)
and the other half represented employees (elected through trade
union representation). The inquiry produced some of the first
research into CORPORATE GOVERNANCE in the UK (although
the subject had yet to be given that title). The Bullock Report recommended the continuation of the British UNITARY BOARD,
but with a proportion of the directors elected, through the trade
union machinery, to represent employee concerns. Business interests were highly critical of both the proposals and the EC

draft fifth directive. Neither has been enacted. However, worker representation through WORKS COUNCILS is gradually being achieved under the Social Chapter of the Maastricht treaty.

Business Roundtable

An association of CEOs in the United States, which has been interested in governance matters for many years. In 2002, following the ENRON debacle, the Business Roundtable (BRT) published new *Principles of Corporate Governance*. These emphasised that, for successful governance, the CEO should be a person of integrity, senior management should set a strong ethical tone "at the top" and there should be a code of conduct, which should enable employees to report potential misconduct without fear of retribution.

www.brtable.org, www.coso.org

Cadbury Report

Prominent institutions in the City of London, concerned about AUDIT and regulatory issues following a number of dramatic company collapses in the 1980s, set up a committee chaired by Sir Adrian Cadbury. To avoid the potential domination of companies by over-powerful chief executives or over-enthusiastic executive management, the committee's 1992 report, *The Financial Aspects of Corporate Governance*, advocated the following checks and balances at board level:

- wider use of independent NON-EXECUTIVE DIRECTORS;
- the introduction of an AUDIT COMMITTEE;
- a separation between CHAIRMAN and CEO;
- the use of remuneration committees;
- adherence to a detailed code of best practice.

Under the code, all UK listed companies were required to report to SHAREHOLDERS on their governance practices, with the ultimate threat of delisting for non-compliance.

The lesson from the Cadbury Report is that greater disclosure is starting to force more careful consideration by the board of company performance, internal management and financial control issues, the setting of strategic goals and companies' competitive positions.
Accountancy, London, May 1997

Reactions to the Cadbury Report varied. Some argued that it lacked teeth, claiming that delisting, being the ultimate sanction, would disadvantage the very shareholders the report set out to protect, and that nothing short of legislation would stop abuses by dominant company leaders. Others feared that giving non-executives more power (Cadbury recommended that they appoint their own leader, have access to legal advice and meet separately if necessary) would erode the concept of the UNITARY BOARD, creating the continental European TWO-TIER BOARD by the back door. In the event, most LISTED COMPANIES decided to comply with the code of best practice, except in the requirement to create NOMINATING COMMITTEES of independent OUTSIDE DIRECTORS to recommend names for board appointment. Cadbury was subsequently incorporated into the UK COMBINED CODE.

C

CalPERS

The Californian State Employees Pension Fund (CalPERS) has been the most proactive institutional investor in the United States, setting a trend in SHAREHOLDER ACTIVISM throughout the country. Now its attention has turned to CORPORATE GOVERNANCE in the international arena. It published a set of global principles for corporate governance in December 1996: "All markets should develop an appropriate code of best practice, by which directors can regulate themselves ... Such a code should be representative of the best governance practice in the market." CalPERS has also proposed principles for good governance in Germany and Japan, arguing that changes are necessary if those countries are to attract overseas capital. CalPERS, however, lost money on its investment in ENRON. (See SHAREHOLDER POWER.)

www.calpers.com

Catalyst

One of the roles a director can play (see CONFORMANCE ROLES).

Cecil King clause

Acting in line with the company's ARTICLES OF ASSOCIATION, the board of International Publishing Corporation in 1968 removed their CHAIRMAN, Cecil King. Since then such provisions in a company's articles have been called Cecil King clauses. Many company articles now include such clauses, sometimes requiring unanimity from the other board members, sometimes only a majority. Despite such provisions, some argue that it is still difficult to remove an underperforming director. To achieve the necessary support, other directors have to declare their position, which could put their own tenure in jeopardy.

C

CEO

Short for chief executive officer, the top member of the management hierarchy. The term, originating in the United States, is now widely used around the world in place of the British alternative, the managing director. In a UNITARY BOARD, the CEO is typically a member of the board. In the United States, contrary to the advice of many CODES OF BEST PRACTICE in CORPORATE GOVERNANCE, the CEO is often also the CHAIRMAN of the board. (see DUALITY.)

> *Britain's captains of industry are programmed early in life with a powerful need to achieve, high levels of resentment and a hunger for others' approval. Reared by dominant mothers who lavish them with tenderness and withdraw their love at the first sign of failure, (they) are brimming with repressed anger and driven by an unconscious craving for affection.*
>
> Cyril Levicki, Reading University, in a study of directors of top UK companies, 2001

Chaebol

Large conglomerate groups of companies in South Korea, dominated by family interests, formed after the second world war with close government involvement. Even though it had only a small shareholding, a family could maintain control by using cross-ownership in subsidiary companies. In recent years, the South Korean government has sought to reduce the power of the *chaebol* by requiring them to divest some of their interests. It had little success before the financial and economic crisis of 1997. Subsequently, the *chaebol*, finding it difficult to compete with other Asian producers because of their tradition of lifetime employment and militant trade unions, had such changes forced on them.

The role of chairman c. 400 AD:
The Abbot shall call together the whole congregation of the brethren to take council. He shall himself explain the questions at issue. And having had the advice of the brethren, he shall think it over himself, and shall do what he considers most advantageous.
Saint Benedict, *Rules for Monks*

Chairman

Many people speak loosely of the chairman of the company, whereas his or her role is, strictly, that of chairman of the company's board of directors. Subject to anything in the company's ARTICLES OF ASSOCIATION, the directors appoint one of their number to take the chair at their meetings; there are few statutory requirements for the role. Consequently, a range of styles is found. At one extreme, the chairman does no more than manage the meetings, arrange the AGENDA, steer the discussions and ensure they reach a conclusion. At the other extreme is the powerful chairman who acts as a figurehead for the company, influences its strategic direction and manages the board, being concerned with its membership, committees and overall performance as well as chairing BOARD MEETINGS. In the UK, the Institute of Directors believes that holding multiple chairmanships is undesirable.

It's never nice serving on a board where the chairman would like you to go.
Dame Vivien Duffield, benefactor and director of the Royal Opera House

The era of political correctness has caused many organisations to reconsider the title of the chairman of their GOVERNING BODY and its committees. Lady chairman, chairwoman, chairperson, or even the name of a piece of furniture, the chair, is used. Worldwide, the number of women chairing the boards of major companies is minimal; but in many charitable and other non-profit companies women play a significant board role.

Whether the role of chairman should be combined with that of the CEO is much debated. Most CODES OF BEST PRACTICE recommend separation; in the United States the roles are often combined (see DUALITY).

I am pleased to see the demise of "chairperson", which has a deathly ring of political correctness. I'm not keen on "chair". The best choice is chairman which, like manhole, does not require feminising. However, those who enjoy gallant gestures might like to use the elegant epithet "Madam Chairman".

John Morgan, writing on modern manners in *The Times*, London, 1998

Chinese corporate governance

In a country influenced by Marxist philosophy, ownership is not the obvious basis for power. Some state enterprises have been turned into corporate entities and floated on the stock-markets in Shanghai and Shenzen. Of the just over 1,200 companies listed in China's A-SHARE market, most are state companies in which the public have minority holdings, 100 or so are collectives, run like PUBLIC COMPANIES ("red hats" in local parlance), and under 100 are privately owned. About one-third of the shares are traded, the rest being held by state bodies. Foreigners were barred from holding A-shares until 2002, when "qualified foreign institutional investors" were allowed by the China Securities Regulatory Commission (CSRC) to buy non-tradable shares to inject foreign capital and expertise. A few Mainland Chinese companies have been listed in Hong Kong and other stock exchanges around the world, after DUE DILIGENCE studies on their financial standing. Others have listed through the back door in Hong Kong by acquiring a LISTED COMPANY and putting a China business into this shell.

Boards of Chinese Mainland-based companies have to cope with multiple lines of control from various Chinese authorities: the relevant industry ministry in Beijing, the People's Bank of China, tax and regulatory bodies, and state, provincial and industry officials, who wish to avoid unacceptable economic and social stresses, including unemployment, bankruptcy, corruption, financial pressures on the state economy and undesirable competition with state enterprises. The CSRC has produced a set of CORPORATE GOVERNANCE standards, but has trouble in effectively enforcing them. In 2001, it required listed companies to have at least two independent NON-EXECUTIVE DIRECTORS, but found that there was a lack of suitable people.

The corporate governance systems in Hong Kong have developed from UK company law and are among the most advanced in Asia. Most companies listed on the Hong Kong Stock Exchange are FAMILY COMPANIES, with control firmly kept within the family. Although the Hong Kong regulatory authorities require a minimum of two non-executive directors, the heads of many family companies see little value in them. Their secretive, authoritarian, family-centred approach to business does not lend itself to OUTSIDE DIRECTORS who might disagree with their decisions. Incidentally, most Hong Kong listed companies are incorporated in Bermuda or the Cayman Islands, so that although Hong Kong's LISTING RULES and takeover code apply, its company law does not.

People who defend bad corporate governance on the grounds of Asian values or some cultural difference are talking nonsense. Yes, there is a different structure of ownership; it's somewhat Victorian in that most companies are family controlled, but had I been around in Victorian times in England I think I would have seen similar bad corporate governance.

David Webb, www.webb-site.com

Circuit breaker

After the 1987 stockmarket crash, some stock exchanges introduced trading breaks. These are points at which trading would be suspended should the market fall a certain distance (350 and 550 points on the New York Stock Exchange) to give time for reflection, avoid panic selling and prevent prices going into free fall. Subsequent experience has led to other ways of triggering the circuit breaker being proposed, such as when the market falls a certain percentage.

Classified boards

See STAGGERED BOARDS.

Closely held company

A PRIVATE COMPANY in which the SHAREHOLDERS and directors are effectively the same people. Consequently, many of the CORPORATE GOVERNANCE checks and balances that are needed to protect the rights of shareholders, where there is a separation between ownership and management, are unnecessary. In some jurisdictions such companies are exempt from some AUDIT, DISCLOSURE and filing requirements. (See FAMILY DIRECTOR.)

Coalition building

See GAMES DIRECTORS PLAY.

Codes of best practice

In the late 1980s, CORPORATE GOVERNANCE practices came under review, following corporate collapses around the world which were blamed on poor board-level practices. Various reports appeared, recommending best practices in corporate governance. The first was the UK's CADBURY REPORT, followed by Australia's HILMER REPORT, France's VIÉNOT REPORT, the Netherlands' PETER REPORT, South Africa's KING REPORT and others. Most proposals were based on perceived good practice rather than rigorous research into their likely effect. In the UK, the Cadbury Report was followed by the Greenbury Report on DIRECTORS' REMUNERATION, the

HAMPEL REPORT and the TURNBULL REPORT on risk assessment. These reports were incorporated in the UK COMBINED CODE (see Appendix 1).

Subsequently, the Commonwealth Secretariat and the World Bank published a set of international principles for corporate governance (see COMMONWEALTH PRINCIPLES FOR CORPORATE GOVERNANCE). The OECD also produced a set of principles of corporate governance for the governments of member states (see Appendix 2).

For details of some codes, visit www.ecgi.org

The difficulty lies, not in the new ideas, but in escaping from the old ones.
John Maynard Keynes, 1936

Co-determination

A governance process adopted in some continental European countries to ensure that significant corporate decisions are taken in partnership between labour and capital. For example, the SUPERVISORY BOARD in the German TWO-TIER BOARD has equal numbers of SHAREHOLDER and employee representatives. Under the Social Chapter of the Maastricht treaty, large multinationals have had to establish WORKS COUNCILS to inform and consult with their employees about strategic changes affecting employment. This has applied in the UK since 1997. From 2005, any firm with 150 or more staff will have to inform and consult about employment prospects; and in 2008 this right will be extended to firms with 50 or more employees.

Combined Code

The CODE OF BEST PRACTICE now adopted in the UK, combining the recommendations of the CADBURY REPORT, the Greenbury report and the HAMPEL REPORT (see Appendix 1). Adopted by the London Stock exchange as a listing requirement, firms must either comply or report the reasons for non-compliance. The subsequent TURNBULL REPORT has also been incorporated.

Commonwealth Principles for Corporate Governance

The Commonwealth Secretariat and the World Bank published a set of principles for CORPORATE GOVERNANCE in 1999, intended to improve the quality of corporate governance in member states of the Commonwealth.

The 15 principles state that the board should:

1 exercise leadership, enterprise, integrity and judgment in directing the corporation so as to achieve continuing prosperity for the corporation and to act in the best interests of the business enterprise in a manner based on transparency, ACCOUNTABILITY and responsibility;

2 ensure that through a managed and effective process board appointments are made that provide a mix of proficient directors, each of whom is able to add value and to bring independent judgment to bear on the decision-making process;

3 determine the corporation's purpose and values, determine the strategy to achieve its purpose and to implement its values to ensure that it survives and thrives, and ensure that procedures and practices are in place that protect the corporation's assets and reputation;

4 monitor and evaluate the implementation of strategies, policies, management performance criteria and business plans;

5 ensure that the corporation complies with all relevant laws, regulations and codes of best business practice;

6 ensure that the corporation communicates with SHAREHOLDERS and other STAKEHOLDERS effectively;

7 serve the legitimate interests of the shareholders of the corporation and account to them fully;

8 identify the firm's internal and external stakeholders and agree a policy, or policies, determining how the corporation should relate to them;

9 ensure that no one person or block of persons has unfettered power and that there is an appropriate balance of power and authority on the board which is, *inter alia*, usually reflected by separating the roles of the chief executive and CHAIRMAN, and by having a balance between executive and NON-EXECUTIVE DIRECTORS;

C

10 regularly review processes and procedures to ensure the effectiveness of its internal systems of control, so that its decision-making capability and the accuracy of its reporting and financial systems are maintained at a high level at all times;

11 regularly assess its performance and effectiveness as a whole, and that of the individual directors, including the chief executive officer;

12 appoint the chief executive officer and at least participate in the appointment of senior management, ensure the motivation and protection of intellectual capital intrinsic to the corporation, ensure that there is adequate training in the corporation for management and employees, and a succession plan for senior management;

13 ensure that all technology and systems used in the corporation are adequate to properly run the business and for it to remain a meaningful competitor;

14 identify key risk areas and key performance indicators of the business enterprise and monitor these factors;

15 ensure annually that the corporation will continue as a going concern for its next fiscal year.

The countries belonging to the Commonwealth are Antigua and Barbuda, Australia, Bahamas, Bangladesh, Barbados, Belize, Botswana, Brunei Darussalam, Cameroon, Canada, Cyprus, Dominica, Fiji, The Gambia, Ghana, Grenada, Guyana, India, Jamaica, Kenya, Kiribati, Lesotho, Malawi, Malaysia, Maldives, Malta, Mauritius, Mozambique, Namibia, Nauru, New Zealand, Nigeria, Pakistan, Papua New Guinea, St Kitts and Nevis, St Lucia, St Vincent and the Grenadines, Samoa, Seychelles, Sierra Leone, Singapore, Solomon Islands, South Africa, Sri Lanka, Swaziland, Tanzania, Tonga, Trinidad and Tobago, Tuvalu, Uganda, UK, Vanuatu, Zambia, Zimbabwe.

Company

See JOINT STOCK LIMITED LIABILITY COMPANY.

Company limited by guarantee

A type of CORPORATE ENTITY in which the guarantors agree to subscribe, should the company be wound up, to the extent of their guarantee given on incorporation. This form of company is adopted for NON-PROFIT ENTITIES, such as academic and educational bodies, cultural and sports organisations, and welfare and other charitable bodies. Network Rail Limited, the company that took over from Railtrack as owner of the UK's railway infrastructure, was incorporated as a "not-for-dividend" company limited by guarantee. Often the amounts guaranteed are nominal and do not expose the members to significant financial liability. In the JOINT STOCK LIMITED LIABILITY COMPANY, by contrast, SHAREHOLDERS' liability is limited to the extent of their equity stake. However, like all corporate entities, companies limited by guarantee need governing – and governing well.

Company secretary

An officer of the company who can, potentially, make an important contribution to the board. As the CADBURY REPORT suggested:

> The company secretary has a key role to play in ensuring that board procedures are both followed and regularly reviewed. The chairman and the board will look to the company secretary for guidance on what their responsibilities are under the rules and regulations to which they are subject and on how those responsibilities should be discharged. All directors should have access to the advice and services of the company secretary and should recognise that the chairman is entitled to the strong support of the company secretary in ensuring the effective functioning of the board.

In the United States, the company secretary is known as the corporate secretary. The American Society of Corporate Secretaries suggests that their duties and responsibilities include organising meetings of the board, board committees and SHAREHOLDERS, maintaining the corporate records and stock

C

(shareholder) records and liaising with the securities markets. It further states that the company secretary should be "the primary liaison between the corporation's directors and management". The company secretary need not be an employee of the company; he or she may work for an outside agency or partnership. Indeed, in some jurisdictions, another company can fulfil the function. In other countries, including Australia, the company secretary must be a person and cannot be a company.

The evolution of the company secretary's role highlights the current contribution. When the JOINT STOCK LIMITED LIABILITY COMPANY was developed in the UK in the mid-19th century, the directors needed someone to keep their records. This was the job of the secretary to the board. The function was largely clerical, with the directors holding the power.

Changing attitudes to company secretaries can be seen in the contrasting comments of two senior British judges. In 1887 Lord Esher, Master of the Rolls, said:

> A secretary is a mere servant. His position is that he is to do what he is told and no person can assume that he has the authority to represent anything at all, nor can anyone assume that statements made by him are necessarily accepted as trustworthy without further enquiry.

A century later things had changed. Corporate life had become complicated. Many companies ran diverse enterprises through complex groups of subsidiary and associated companies. Legislation affecting companies has become substantial. Now the role of the company secretary calls for professional knowledge and skill. In 1971 Lord Denning, Master of the Rolls, said:

> Times have changed. A company secretary is a much more important person nowadays than he was in 1871. He is an officer of the company with extensive duties and responsibilities. This appears not only in modern Companies Acts but also in the role which he plays in the day-to-day business of companies. He is no longer merely a clerk. He regularly makes representations on behalf of the company and enters into contracts on its behalf ... so much so that he may be

regarded as held out to do such things on behalf of the company. He is certainly entitled to sign contracts connected with the administrative side of the company's affairs, such as employing staff, ordering cars and so forth. All such matters come within the ostensible authority of a company secretary.

www.icsa.org.uk, www.icsasoftware.com

Compensation committee

Another name for REMUNERATION COMMITTEE.

Confidant

One of the roles a director can play (see next entry).

Conformance roles

There are two principal sets of roles that every UNITARY BOARD of directors and GOVERNING BODY must fulfil (see Figure 3 on page 4): the conformance roles, involving EXECUTIVE SUPERVISION and ACCOUNTABILITY, and the PERFORMANCE ROLES, involving strategy formulation and policymaking. Many of the CODES OF BEST PRACTICE in CORPORATE GOVERNANCE emphasise the conformance roles; indeed, the HILMER REPORT specifically criticises the underemphasis on performance roles.

The main conformance roles can be thought of as follows.

Judge Directors playing this role are able to make an objective assessment of a situation. This can be a vital contribution of the OUTSIDE DIRECTOR, who, obviously, has the opportunity to see board matters from an external and independent point of view. Such an objective evaluation of senior management performance can overcome the tunnel vision sometimes found in those too closely involved with the situation, or the myopia brought on by being personally affected by the outcome.

C

Catalyst This role is played by a director who is capable of questioning the board's assumptions, causing change in others' thinking. Catalysts point out that what appears to be an incontrovertible truth to some board members is, in fact, rooted in questionable beliefs that others have about the company, its markets, its competitors and so on. They highlight inferences that are masquerading as facts and indicate when value judgments, rather than rigorous analysis, are being used in board deliberations. Most valuably, catalysts stimulate the board discussions with new insights and ideas.

Supervisor The whole board is responsible for the monitoring and supervision of executive management. But the calls for NON-EXECUTIVE DIRECTORS, for a separation of the chairmanship from the chief executive responsibility and for the use of AUDIT, NOMINATING and REMUNERATION COMMITTEES emphasise the value of the supervisor role of outside directors.

Watchdog Directors who cast themselves in this role see themselves as protectors of the interests of other parties, such as the SHAREHOLDERS or, more often, a specific interest group. REPRESENTATIVE or NOMINEE DIRECTORS inevitably find themselves in this position, as they look out for the interests of the party who put them on the board. This might be a major investor for a director on the board of an American or British LISTED COMPANY, the employees for a director on a German SUPERVISORY BOARD, or the *keiretsu* group interests for a director on the board of a major Japanese company (see JAPANESE CORPORATE GOVERNANCE). Every director has a duty to be concerned with the interests of the company as a whole (that is, with the interests of all the members without discrimination), so the watchdog role should be applied with care.

Confidant Some directors may find themselves acting as a sounding board for other directors, the CEO or the CHAIRMAN; as a trusted and respected counsellor in times of uncertainty and stress; or as someone to share concerns with about issues (often interpersonal problems) outside the boardroom. Political process at board level inevitably involves the use, and sometimes abuse, of power; the confidant can make a valuable contribution. But it is vital that he or she commands the trust of all the directors, otherwise the problem may be reinforced rather than resolved.

Safety valve It is a legitimate role for directors to act as safety valves at a time of crisis, in order to release the pressure, prevent further damage and save the situation. A classical example would be when the company has run into financial problems, management performance has deteriorated and the chief executive has to be replaced. Another example might be if the company faced an unexpected catastrophe. The sensible and steadying counsel of a wise member of the board could save an otherwise disastrous situation.

Contact person

One of the roles a director can play (see PERFORMANCE ROLES).

Cooking the books

Once the preserve of overenthusiastic accountants, the falsification of records and the manipulation of financial results have reached the boardroom in some prominent companies. Directors of the following companies were all involved in what some of them, euphemistically, called 'aggressive earnings management' and others saw as financial manipulation.

- ENRON, apparently a highly successful American energy trader, engineered a set of special purpose entities which took massive debts off its balance sheet.
- INDEPENDENT INSURANCE COMPANY, an entrepreneurial British insurance company, simply failed to enter huge claims in its accounts.
- WORLDCOM, a massive American telecoms firm, capitalised $3.8 billion of maintenance costs, which should have been charged against profits, as fixed assets to be written off over time.
- Elan, an Irish pharmaceuticals group, sold the rights to royalties to companies it had created, with the option to buy them back at higher prices.
- SUNBEAM, an American appliances manufacturer,

shipped more goods to distributors than they could possibly sell, taking credit for the revenue but ignoring returned goods.

Boards of LISTED COMPANIES are always under pressure from INSTITUTIONAL INVESTORS to show healthy profits and growth. As a result, some are tempted to misrepresent their company's results. Those who have SHARE OPTIONS that have become exercisable (or will soon do so) will also be keen for the results to look good and for the share price to rise.

Core capability

See next entry.

Core competence

The hidden strengths of a business that the directors can call on during STRATEGY FORMULATION. Unlike the more obvious resources that a company has, such as its product portfolio, its finances and its organisational characteristics, core competencies reflect the knowledge in the organisation and its learning capability. A core competence in a financial institution might be its strength in handling derivatives, in a software house its experience in networking applications, or in an automobile manufacturer its knowledge of electronic controls. Some refer to core competencies as core capabilities, broadening the definition to include, for example, the ability of an entertainment company to deliver its video product over cable television, or of a retail chain store to access its suppliers directly by satellite-based electronic data interchange.

Strategic thinking in Western companies in recent years has emphasised the benefits of identifying the core competencies and capabilities of the firm and building on them to the exclusion of all else. This includes not only the divesting of conglomerate businesses unrelated to the core activities, but also outsourcing other functions so that both financial and managerial resources can be concentrated on the activities that are crucial to the company's strategic performance. Asian companies, by and large, do not share this enthusiasm for concentration, seeing business more as a series of trading opportunities, which enable transient networks of intertrading entities to be created, often with CROSS-HOLDINGS and cross-directorships.

Core values

A statement, typically approved at board level, of the underlying beliefs that a company has about itself and its relations with those involved with it. The core values of a passenger transport company, for example, might include statements that it is dedicated to safety, customer service and cost-effective travel, while providing rewarding career opportunities and job satisfaction for its staff and a reasonable reward for its investors. The articulation of core values can influence the process of STRATEGY FORMULATION and POLICYMAKING, not least because it defines the playing field, the games that are to be played and the rules by which the company intends to operate. (See also MISSION STATEMENT and SUSTAINABLE DEVELOPMENT.)

The rise of the modern corporation has brought a concentration of economic power, which can compete on equal terms with the modern state – economic power versus political power, each strong in its own field. The state seeks in some aspects to regulate the corporation, while the corporation, steadily becoming more powerful, makes every effort to avoid such regulation.
Adolf Berle and Gardiner Means, 1932

Corporate entity

The development of the corporate concept in the middle of the 19th century enabled massive capital formation, dramatic industrial development and untold wealth creation around the world. Previously, the only way to organise business was as a sole trader or partnership, in which, if the business failed, the debtor went to prison and his family to the poorhouse. The JOINT STOCK LIMITED LIABILITY COMPANY enabled a legal entity to be incorporated with an existence separate from its owners, whose liability for the company's debts was limited to their equity stake. Such a corporate entity can contract, sue and be sued, independently of those who have provided the capital. A dramatically simple and superbly successful concept originally, the notion of corporate entity has now become complex, with many different types of corporate structures, many forms of financial instruments and complicated international corporate networks.

Effective corporate governance ensures that long-term strategic objectives and plans are established and that the proper management and management structure are in place to achieve those objectives, while at the same time making sure that the structure functions to maintain the corporation's integrity, reputation and accountability to its constituencies.

National Association of Corporate Directors, Washington, DC

Corporate governance

The exercise of power over a CORPORATE ENTITY and the overall subject of this book. The process by which companies are directed and controlled, according to the CADBURY REPORT. All corporate entities need to be governed as well as managed. The structure, membership and processes of the GOVERNING BODY, typically the board of directors in a JOINT STOCK LIMITED LIABILITY COMPANY, are central to corporate governance. So is the linkage between the board and senior management. The relationships between the board and the SHAREHOLDERS, the AUDITORS, the REGULATORS and other STAKEHOLDERS are also crucial to effective corporate governance.

The word "governance" is ancient: Chaucer used it, although he spelt in two different ways. But the phrase "corporate governance" is young. The first book with the title *Corporate Governance* was published in 1984, the same year that the

American Institute published a report on the "Principles of Corporate Governance". *Corporate Governance: An International Review*, an academic journal, was launched in 1993.

www.thecorporatelibrary.com, www.ragm.com, www.corpgov.net, www.worldbank.org/html/fpd/privatesector/cg/index.htm, www.oecd.org

C

The corporate governance debate has done little to improve the contribution of many boards. If anything the attention has been switched from building larger and better corporate cakes to applying the boardroom icing to existing cakes in recommended ways.
Colin Coulson-Thomas, 2002

Corporate governance policies

See BOARD CORPORATE GOVERNANCE POLICIES.

The proper governance of companies will become as important as the proper governance of countries.
James D. Wolfensohn, president, World Bank

Governance ratings are becoming the leading edge of the corporate governance movement. Ultimately such ratings will play a similar role in the equity market as credit ratings currently do in the bond market.
Steven Davis, Davis Global Advisers, 2001

Corporate governance ratings

Various organisations have rating systems and keep scorecards on companies' performance. These include INSTITUTIONAL INVESTORS such as CALPERS and HERMES INVESTMENT MANAGEMENT and investigating firms such as Davis Global Advisers in the United States, PIRC and Déminor in Europe, and CLSA Emerging Markets. Broadly, markets pay a premium for shares that are well rated on their CORPORATE GOVERNANCE policies and practice.

www.calpers.com, www.davisglobal.com, www.clsa.com, www.deminor.org, www.hermes.co.uk, www.pirc.co.uk

C

Corporate monitoring

Proposals for making corporate management more accountable to a company's SHAREHOLDERS, to increase stock returns, to control CEOs' pay and to balance profits with social goals by encouraging minority shareholders to use their VOTING RIGHTS. Following warnings about self-serving company directors, financial analysts pushing shares and less than independent AUDITORS, the founder of this project, Mark Latham, proposes the use of proxy advisory firms, paid for by the company, that would give independent voting advice to shareholders.

www.corpmon.com

Corporate planning

An analytical and professional approach to the board's PERFORMANCE ROLES. Growing competition around the world during the 1960s meant firms could no longer sell all they could produce. A market-oriented professionalism began to emerge. Management consultants offered analytical tools, such as PORTFOLIO ANALYSIS, product mapping, scenario building, SWOT ANALYSIS and value-chain analysis (see ADDED-VALUE CHAIN). Corporate planning departments were created. Directors were drawn into the strategic thinking process.

Corporate senate

Modelled on the successful Spanish Mondragon worker co-operatives, Shann Turnbull has applied the concept to public companies that he has formed in Australia. He suggests that "most corporations in the English-speaking world are essentially corrupt because their UNITARY BOARD structures concentrate on conflicts of interest and corporate power". His alternative is a dual board structure with a corporate senate with no more than three members, elected on the basis of one vote per SHAREHOLDER, not per share. The senate has no proactive power, just the right to veto where it feels the board has a conflict of interest. (See also SHAREHOLDER DEMOCRACY.)

Corporate social responsibility

Initially, the main focus of CORPORATE GOVERNANCE was on protecting SHAREHOLDER interests and maximising long-term shareholder value. Increasingly, however, boards around the world are being called on to recognise the social and environmental impact of their companies' activities. These calls for corporate social responsibility (CSR), sometimes called corporate citizenship, come from international organisations, governments and lobbying organisations, as well as groups with specific agendas. Examples of the issues being pursued include allowing worldwide access to affordable pharmaceuticals, reducing global-warming emissions, labelling genetically engineered food, establishing policies to avoid money laundering and linking board pay with social performance. Traditionally, companies reported corporate performance to their SHAREHOLDERS in financial terms. Now there are calls for broader reporting on CSR performance criteria to wider STAKEHOLDER interests. Some companies do report social and environmental indicators as well as the traditional financial performance measures; this is sometimes known as the triple bottom line. (See also ETHICS and SUSTAINABLE DEVELOPMENT.)

www.eiris.org, www.iccr.org, www.corpwatch.org, www.unglobalcompact.org, www.profitwithprinciple.co.uk, www.AccountAbility.org.uk, www.uksif.org, www.globalreporting.org

Corporate strategy

See STRATEGY FORMULATION.

C

Corporate veil

A legal phrase emphasising that a company whose SHARE-HOLDERS have limited liability is effectively surrounded by a veil which creditors cannot pierce in pursuit of their debts. In common-law jurisdictions, this even applies to subsidiary companies that are wholly owned by a parent company which controls their activities. In other words, the holding company may walk away from its subsidiary's debts. In some other jurisdictions, including Germany, creditors may pursue their debts up the corporate chain of dominating companies in a group, thus piercing the corporate veil.

Corporatisation

See PRIVATISATION.

Country-club board

See BOARD STYLES.

Crony capitalism

It was suggested that the economic shocks that hit East Asia in late 1997 were caused by CORPORATE GOVERNANCE based on close links between directors and members of government, the ruling elite or business associates, rather than on sound business logic. This contrasted with the alternative explanation of previous business success based on ASIAN VALUES.

Cronyism

See GAMES DIRECTORS PLAY.

Cross-directorships

See INTERLOCKING DIRECTORSHIPS.

Cross-holding

The holding of voting shares by one company in another. The practice is prevalent in East Asia, where many companies build networks of alliances and share risk. Cross-directorships (INTERLOCKING DIRECTORSHIPS) are often found where there are cross-holdings of shares. Some jurisdictions prohibit a subsidiary company holding shares in its parent, so that the device cannot be used to prevent a hostile takeover bid and thwart the MARKET FOR CONTROL. (See also JAPANESE CORPORATE GOVERNANCE.)

Crown jewels

A takeover defence used by some boards of companies targeted in a hostile takeover bid, in which they contract with another party to license or acquire a right in significant company assets. The aim is to reduce the attractiveness of the company to predators. The terms of such an arrangement often allow the other party to buy out the company at a predetermined price should the takeover materialise, or obtain damages in lieu.

D&O insurance

See INDEMNITY INSURANCE.

Deal making

See GAMES DIRECTORS PLAY.

Deep-pocket syndrome

When a company is in financial difficulty or has become insolvent, there may be little point in SHAREHOLDERS or creditors suing the company because it has no money. Instead, their best option is to take legal actions against those who are covered by INDEMNITY INSURANCE, such as directors and, particularly, the company AUDITORS, to pay them what they are legally owed by the company. (See also LITIGATION.)

Dematerialisation

The process of replacing the title to shares, traditionally recognised with hard-copy share certificates, by electronic means. It enables the electronic transfer of title, without the cumbersome tracing, handling and exchanging pieces of paper. In an electronic share transfer system, SHAREHOLDERS give their authority to a company-sponsored share nominee. Dematerialisation is practised in the United States. In the UK, full dematerialisation has proved elusive, because some shareholders still insist on holding formal share certificates, even though they often lose them. In the rest of Europe it is hampered by the existence of bearer shares, which do not have a nominated owner.

Descent from heaven

Amakaduri, literally in Japanese a descent from heaven, refers to the practice, once prevalent in some major Japanese companies, of appointing retiring bureaucrats from the regulatory bodies to well-paid sinecures, including directorships, when they retired. The same process can be seen in other countries, including France, where members of the *grandes écoles* fraternity move readily from government to corporate service. (See REGULATORY CAPTURE.)

D

Director

A member of the board of directors formally nominated and appointed by the SHAREHOLDERS in a properly convened meeting of the company in accordance with its ARTICLES OF ASSOCIATION. Some people may have a title including the word director – marketing director, director of administration, regional director and so on – without necessarily being formal members of the board. Such titles are sometimes given as rewards or to add status to executives in their dealings with the outside world. Such directors, unless they present themselves as actual directors, have none of the responsibilities or any of the rights of legally appointed directors. (See ASSOCIATE DIRECTOR.)

www.boardroomanalysis.com

The pleasant but vacuous director need never worry about job security.
Warren Buffett, chairman, Berkshire Hathaway Fund

Directors' contracts

The Greenbury Report criticised the practice of giving directors rolling contracts of three or more years and proposed that they should run for no more than a year. This meant that directors who performed poorly and were replaced did not receive a massive GOLDEN HANDSHAKE on the termination of a long-term contract. However, the basis of contracts for CEOs remains a subject of debate in the United States and the UK, particularly when incompetence sometimes seems to be richly rewarded. (See DIRECTORS' REMUNERATION.)

Directors' duties

The British government's company law review, published in 2002 (and obviously drafted by a lawyer), proposed the following set of functions for directors.

1 Compliance and loyalty

a A director must exercise his powers honestly and for their proper purpose, and in accordance with the company's constitution and decisions taken lawfully under it.

b Subject to that requirement, he must (so far as he practically can) exercise his powers in the way he believes in good faith is best calculated in the circumstances, taking account of both the short- and the long-term consequences of his acts, to promote the success of the company for the benefit of its members as a whole.

c The circumstances to which he is to have regard for that purpose include, in particular (as his duties of care and skill may require):

- the company's need to foster its business relationships, including those with its employees, suppliers and customers for its products and services;
- the impact of its operations on the communities affected and on the environment; and
- its need to maintain a reputation for high standards of business conduct.

2 Independence of judgment

a A director must not (except as lawfully permitted under the company's constitution) restrict his power to exercise an independent judgment.

b But this does not prevent him doing anything to carry out an agreement entered into in accordance with his duties.

3 Conflict of interest

A director must not:

a authorise, procure or permit the company to enter into any transaction in which he has an interest unless the interest has been disclosed to the relevant directors to the extent required under the Companies Act; or

b use any property, INFORMATION or opportunity of the

company for his own or anyone else's benefit, or obtain a benefit in any other way in connection with the exercise of his powers, unless he is allowed to make such use or obtain such benefit by the company's constitution, or the use or benefit has been disclosed to the company in general meeting and the company has consented to it.

D

4 Fairness
A director must act fairly as between the company's members.

5 Care, skill and diligence
A director must exercise the care, skill and diligence which should be exercised by a reasonably diligent person with both the knowledge, skill and experience which may reasonably be expected of a director in his position and any additional knowledge, skill and experience which he has.

www.dti.gov.uk/cld/review.htm

Directors' liability

Misunderstanding about the liability of directors abounds. Unlike SHAREHOLDERS, directors' liability is not limited by the incorporation of a JOINT STOCK LIMITED LIABILITY COMPANY. Directors are not automatically liable for the debts of their company, provided they have not acted negligently or made it appear that they accepted personal liability. But a director can be personally liable for the firm's debts if he or she knew that the company was insolvent and allowed it to continue to trade. Disqualification from serving as a director can result (see DISQUALIFICATION OF DIRECTORS). Directors can also be fined if they mislead AUDITORS or fail to file various documents with the companies' registrar.

www.companieshouse.co.uk

Directors' remuneration

This remains a hot topic. INSTITUTIONAL INVESTORS in the

United States and the UK have, for some years, been challenging the remuneration packages available to some directors, particularly when they seem to reward failure. In 1995 a group of City of London institutions commissioned Sir Richard Greenbury, then CHAIRMAN of Marks and Spencer, to look into board-level pay. The Greenbury Report provided a Code of Conduct which has now been incorporated in the UK COMBINED CODE. The main recommendations were:

- that companies should create REMUNERATION COMMITTEES consisting solely of independent NON-EXECUTIVE DIRECTORS;
- that the chairman of the remuneration committee should respond to SHAREHOLDERS' questions at the AGM;
- that annual reports should include details of all director rewards, naming each director;
- that directors' contracts should run for no more than a year to avoid excessive GOLDEN HANDSHAKES; and
- that SHARE OPTION schemes for directors should be linked to long-term corporate performance.

"Performance and Integrity – How We Reward Our Leaders" (title of a booklet published by pharmaceutical giant GlaxoSmithKline). A title such as this, that seeks to justify astonishing increases to an already astonishingly generous pay package, echoes Orwell's Ministry of Truth.
Sunday Times, November 2002

However, the code has not reduced claims of excessive remuneration, sometimes for failure on a massive scale. In 2003 the ASSOCIATION OF BRITISH INSURERS and the NATIONAL ASSOCIATION OF PENSION FUNDS jointly published a practice statement on how boards should avoid unmerited severance payments. Performance objectives for executives should be clear so there is no need for compensation for those who have failed. Pension enhancements for departing executives should be justified to shareholders. (See also DIRECTORS' REMUNERATION REPORT and REMUNERATION RATCHETING.)

We need to bury the myth that executive incentives align managers' interests with those of their shareholders. Incentives always reward exceptional performance or exceptional deception: in most cases deception is the easier route.
David Creelman, 2002

D

I have raised the matter of boardroom pay at every company of which I have ever been a director. My stance has always been that it is wrong to award directors, say, 17% while giving the workforce 2% ...
The usual answer is that "it is the market. We need to pay that money to recruit/retain/motivate top talent".
Well I don't see too many vacancies in the boardroom.
Prue Leith, cookery expert, business woman and non-executive director

The going rate for a non-executive (of a major listed company) is £30,000 a year. I don't know by how much this should be increased, but in America the rate is about £75,000.
Paul Myners, former head of Gartmore Securities and author of the Myners Report

Directors' remuneration report

Legislation in the UK, applicable from the start of 2003, requires quoted companies to publish directors' remuneration reports and put them to the SHAREHOLDERS' vote at the AGM. The report must contain:

- details of the members of the REMUNERATION COMMITTEE and anyone who advised that committee;
- a statement of the company's policy on directors' remuneration for the future;
- details of individual directors' remuneration, including the performance criteria in incentive schemes, pensions and retirement benefits, and their service contracts;
- a line graph for the past five years showing how the company's performance has compared with competitors.

Although shareholders vote on the report, the outcome remains advisory. However, the withdrawal of exceedingly generous remuneration proposals, following opposition from a significant body of shareholders (at GlaxoSmithKline and Prudential in the UK, for example) suggests that the idea of shareholders' influence can work.

D In the United States, all LISTED COMPANIES are required to report details of directors' remuneration to the SECURITIES AND EXCHANGE COMMISSION, where the information is publicly available and accessible through the internet.

Directors' report and accounts

Almost all company law jurisdictions now require the directors to submit regular reports and accounts to all shareholders (the exceptions are generally tax havens such as the British Virgin Islands). The form and content of such reports and accounts have been progressively widened and sharpened through company law and by regulatory requirements, such as those of the American SECURITIES AND EXCHANGE COMMISSION, the Australian Securities Commission and the Hong Kong Securities and Futures Commission.

www.standardandpoors.com

Transparency and good corporate governance
do not come naturally to people.
Frances Reid, European Bank for Reconstruction and Development, 2002

Disclosure

Directors have a FIDUCIARY DUTY not to make a SECRET PROFIT out of their position as a director. For example, a director or a close member of his or her family might be involved with another company that was bidding for a contract or have a personal interest in a company being considered for acquisition. Any such interest must be disclosed before the director takes part in any board decision-making on the matter. The CHAIRMAN and fellow directors can then decide on the appropriate action, such as asking the director to leave the meeting or not participate in the discussion, or, having noted the interest, allowing participation in the decision-making. Directors should ensure that any interest declared is minuted, in case there is a subsequent legal challenge.

D

> *Cleverness, high salaries and impressive job titles*
> *do not guarantee full and fair disclosure.*
> Colin Coulson-Thomas, 2002

Disqualification of directors

Most company law jurisdictions provide for the disqualification of directors if they are unfit to serve. Causes include theft, fraud, failure to meet the requirements of the companies' legislation, or running a company that has traded while insolvent and without a reasonable chance of paying its creditors.

www.uk.experian.com

> *You cannot legislate for honesty in the boardroom.*
> Cahal Dowds, president, Institute of Chartered Accountants of Scotland, 2002

Divide and rule

See GAMES DIRECTORS PLAY.

> *The board's real role is to support the leader – whoever he is, chairman*
> *or CEO. If my board was absolutely divided I would put the matter to a*
> *vote: but all those who vote against me should resign.*
> The opinion of a dominant director

Dominant director

Sometimes a company reflects the entrepreneurial drive of one person, often the founder. In such cases, the dominant director often overshadows the board, although directors are able to offer advice, which might be heeded. (Bill Gates of Microsoft and Richard Branson of Virgin are examples of highly success-ful dominant corporate leaders.) But although dominant direc-tors may take their companies to the highest levels of achievement, unless they can cope with the succession problem they ultimately fail. The list of those who failed to provide for their succession includes Henry Ford and "Tiny" Rowland of Lonrho. Unfortunately, experience suggests that dominant di-rectors have great difficulty in working with a potential succes-sor – "nothing grows under an oak tree". (See also DUALITY.)

DREXEL, BURNHAM, LAMBERT

A Wall Street securities trading firm that was at the heart of the predatory takeover market in the 1980s, using high-return, high-risk "junk" bonds. It provided the base for the INSIDER DEALING activities of Ivan Boesky and the setting for the nefar-ious activities of Dennis Levine and Michael Milken. Levine, then in his 20s, discovered that insider trading was easy and ap-parently foolproof. In his job he had access to information about prospective financial deals. Exchange that knowledge with an executive in another bank who knew about that bank's deals, trade the shares under a fictitious name in the Bahamas, open an account in a Swiss bank and, bingo, the compliance au-thorities would never know. Later he grew overconfident – some might say greedy. He took a position in a company for which his own company was preparing a bid and made $1.3m. But he underestimated the capabilities of government investiga-tors, acting with the co-operation of securities regulators (see INTERNATIONAL ORGANISATION OF SECURITIES COMMIS-SIONS). Levine pleaded guilty, gave evidence against his col-leagues, and was sentenced to two years' imprisonment and a fine of $362,000. He also had to make restitution to the SECURI-TIES AND EXCHANGE COMMISSION of $11.6m in insider-trading profits and was barred from employment in the securities business for life. Milken was charged with racketeer-ing and securities fraud. He agreed to plead guilty to six felonies, paid $600m in restitution and was sentenced to ten years in prison. One of the effects of these activities was a growing interest in CORPORATE GOVERNANCE. In 1988 Drexel pleaded guilty to six securities felonies and paid a record $650m in restitution. In 1990 it filed for the protection of the Bankruptcy Court.

> *Failed leaders were being revealed in every walk of life ... sad examples of excess, greed, and cynicism. I was profoundly disappointed at how frequently the graduates of some of our finest business and law schools were involved, in one way or another, in the cases being brought before the SEC. Surely we could do better."*
> John Shad, former chairman of the SEC

Dual voting rights

Some jurisdictions forbid companies to issue classes of shares with different VOTING RIGHTS. Some stock exchange LISTING RULES also forbid them. Where they are allowed, shares with different voting rights can be used to preserve the overall power of a founding family or other incumbent interests, when issuing additional shares threatens to dilute their control of the company. (See A AND B SHARES.)

> *The basis for a reliable system of corporate governance is the current CEO-dominant paradigm. The only credible alternative is for large – primarily institutional – shareholders to exert far more control over corporate affairs than they appear willing to exercise. I prefer the benevolent despot.*
> Alan Greenspan, March 2002

Duality

One of the continuing debates about the UNITARY BOARD is whether the role of CHAIRMAN and CEO should be separate or combined. In the United States, most LISTED COMPANIES combine these roles, giving considerable power to the head of the company. In the UK, the CADBURY REPORT advocated separation. In Australia, the roles in PUBLIC COMPANIES are usually separated. The arguments in favour of splitting the roles are that two heads are better than one, but (more importantly) that duality provides essential checks and balances. SHARE-HOLDERS, particularly if there are minority interests, may find that a DOMINANT LEADER, who is both chairman and CEO, has no one to keep him under control. The alternative view is that single-minded leadership can produce better performance. The results of research into the alternatives seems to be that under single leadership a company can do better, at least for a while, but that where the subtle relationship between the chairman and the CEO works well, major companies thrive better in the longer term. An extension of the duality argument is whether a CEO should ever be appointed chairman of the board after retirement. It often happens. Proponents talk of retaining the person's experience; but newly appointed CEOs more typically fear that their predecessor may not be able to let go of the managerial ropes when he occupies the chairmanship.

The classic argument against the chairman being the former CEO is that the chairman will be a meddler. The CEO doesn't need that, of course, but he does need someone to confide in, to talk candidly about changes and other important matters. People in top positions need someone they can talk with openly and honestly.

Warren Bennis, 1993

Due diligence

The process of ensuring that a company's prospectus or similar description of a company's worth is accurate, not misleading and prepared with care. Usually carried out by a firm of professional accountants, due diligence is an essential prerequisite of issuing shares, PRIVATISATION and valuing companies.

Duty of care

Most legal systems impose on directors a duty to exercise reasonable care, diligence and skill in their work, through statute, case law or regulation. Directors are expected to bring to their director-level responsibilities the degree of care that could reasonably be expected, given their qualifications, know-how and experience. The interpretation of what constitutes reasonable care obviously depends on the background of the individual. If a director were a qualified accountant, engineer or lawyer, then the degree of care would take these qualifications into account. But even if they have no such qualifications, the standard of professionalism now expected of directors around the world is significantly higher than it was a few years ago. Courts can act if fraudulent or negligent behaviour is alleged, or where there are apparent abuses of power or suppression of the interests of minority shareholders. For example, courts will give a ruling if it is alleged that the directors have negotiated a contract that is detrimental to the interests of the minority. But, broadly, courts will not act to second-guess board-level business decisions taken under circumstances of normal commercial risk, should they subsequently prove to have been ill judged.

ECGI

See EUROPEAN CORPORATE GOVERNANCE INSTITUTE.

Empire building

See GAMES DIRECTORS PLAY.

Employee director

See WORKER DIRECTOR.

Employee representation

See WORKER DIRECTOR.

Employee Retirement Income Security Act

In the United States, the Employee Retirement Income Security
Act (ERISA) of 1974 lays down fiduciary responsibility rules for
all those who exercise control over the assets of employee retirement benefit plans. The Pension and Welfare Administration, which administers and enforces the act, has laid down
criteria (in the frequently referred to "Avon letter") which
require the fund managers to act in the best interests of SHARE-
HOLDERS and plan beneficiaries, and not to use their proxy
votes in companies in any way that is not in the beneficiaries'
interests. This legislation also prevents directors calling on the
proxy votes of shares held by their company's pension funds to
promote or protect their own positions.

Employee share ownership

Employee share ownership is sometimes advanced as a means

of ensuring employees' commitment. Instead of capital hiring labour, the argument runs, employees use capital. The governance processes of such companies typically involve employee-nominated members. Employee share ownership plans (ESOP) are most advanced in the United States, partly because US tax laws allow ESOPs generous tax relief. In the UK, the John Lewis Partnership is the most frequently cited example of employee ownership.

ENRON

The merger of Houston Natural Gas and InterNorth in 1985 created Enron, a new Texas energy company. In 1989 Enron began trading in commodities, buying and selling wholesale contracts in energy. By 2000, turnover was growing at a fantastic rate, from $40 billion in 1999 to $101 billion in 2000, with the increased revenue coming from the broking of energy commodities. The rapid growth rate suggested a dynamic company, and Enron's share price rocketed. Senior executives reaped large rewards from their share options. The company's bankers, who received substantial fees, also employed the analysts who encouraged others to invest in Enron. But the cash flow statement included an unusual item: other operating activities $1.1 billion. The 2000 accounts were the last Enron was to publish.

Joseph Skilling, Enron's CEO, believed that old asset-based businesses would be dominated by trading enterprises such as Enron making markets for their output. Enron was credited with "aggressive earnings management". To support its growth, hundreds of SPECIAL PURPOSE ENTITIES (SPES) were created. These were separate partnerships that traded with Enron, with names such as Cayman, Condor and Raptor, Jedi and Chewco, often based in tax havens. Enron priced long-term energy supply contracts with these SPES at market prices, taking the profit in its own accounts immediately. The SPES provided lucrative fees for Enron's senior executives. They also made it appear that Enron had hedged its financial exposures with third parties, whereas the third parties were actually contingent liabilities on Enron. The contemporary US accounting standards (GAAP) did not require such SPES to be consolidated with partners' group accounts, so billions of dollars were kept off Enron's balance sheet.

In 2000, Enron's revenue was $100 billion and the company was valued by the stockmarket at nearly $80 billion. It was ranked seventh in *Fortune*'s list of the largest American companies. It then had three principal divisions, with over 3,500 subsidiaries: Enron Global Services, owning physical assets such as power stations and pipelines; Enron Energy Services, providing management and outsourcing services; and Enron Wholesale Services, a commodities and trading business. Enron was the largest trader in the energy market created by the deregulation of energy in the United States.

Warning signs

Enron's AUDITOR was ANDERSEN, whose AUDIT and consultancy fees from the company were running at about $52m a year. It also employed several former Andersen partners as senior financial executives. In February 2001, Andersen partners discussed dropping their client because of its accounting policies, including accounting for the SPES and the apparent conflicts of interest of Andrew Fastow, Enron's chief financial officer, who had set up and was benefiting from the SPES. In August 2001, Skilling resigned "for personal reasons". Kenneth Lay, the CHAIRMAN, took over executive control. Lay was a friend of President George W. Bush and was his adviser on energy matters. His name had been mentioned as a future American energy secretary. In 2000, Lay made $123m from the exercise of SHARE OPTIONS in Enron.

A week after Skilling resigned, Chung Wu, a broker with UBS Paine Webber (a subsidiary of UBS, a Swiss bank) emailed his clients advising them to sell Enron. He was sacked and escorted out of his office. The same day, Lay sold $4m of his own Enron shares, while telling employees of his high priority to restore investor confidence, which "should result in a higher share price". Other UBS analysts were still recommending a "strong buy" on Enron. UBS Paine Webber received substantial brokerage fees from administering the Enron employee stock option programme. Lord Wakeham, a former British cabinet minister, was a director of Enron and chairman of its NOMINATING COMMITTEE. Wakeham, who was also a chartered accountant and chairman of the British Press Complaints Council, was paid an annual consultancy fee of $50,000 by Enron, plus $4,600 per month as retainer and $1,250 as attendance fee for each meeting.

In mid-2001, Lay was given a warning about the company's accounting techniques by Sherron Watkins, an Enron executive, who wrote: "I am nervous that we will implode in a wave of accounting scandals." She also advised Andersen about potential problems. In October 2001 a crisis developed. The company revised its earlier financial statements, revealing massive losses caused by hedging risks taken as energy prices fell, which had wiped out $600m of profits. An SEC investigation into this restatement of profits for the past five years revealed massive, complex derivative positions and the transactions between Enron and the SPEs. Debts were understated by $2.6 billion. Fastow was alleged to have received more than $30m for his management of the partnerships. Eventually, he was indicted on 78 counts involving the complicated financial schemes that produced phantom profits, enriched him and doomed the company. He claimed that he did not believe he had committed any crimes.

BEFORE THE EVENT:

Few companies will be able to achieve the excitement extravaganza that Enron has in its remarkable business transformation, but many could apply some of the principles.

Ed Michaels, Helen Handfield-Jones and Beth Axelrod,
The War for Talent, 2001

The FBI investigates

The FBI began an investigation into possible fraud at Enron three months later, by which time files had been shredded. In a subsequent criminal trial, Andersen was found guilty of destroying key documents as part of an effort to impede an official inquiry into Enron's collapse. Lawsuits against Andersen followed. The Enron employees' pension fund sued for $1 billion, plus the return of $1 million per week fees, seeing the firm as their best chance of recovering some of the $80 billion lost in the debacle. Many Enron employees held their retirement plans in Enron stock; some had lost their entire retirement savings. The Labor Department alleged that Enron had illegally prohibited employees from selling company stock in their 401K retirement plans as the share price fell. Andersen subsequently collapsed; its partnerships around the world joined other BIG FOUR firms.

In November 2001 Fastow was fired. Standard & Poors, a credit-rating agency, downgraded Enron stock to junk-bond status, triggering interest rate penalties and other clauses. Merger negotiations with Dynergy, which might have saved Enron, failed.

Bankruptcy
Enron filed for Chapter 11 bankruptcy in December 2001. This was the largest corporate collapse in American history to that time; WORLDCOM was to surpass it. The New York Stock Exchange (NYSE) suspended Enron shares. John Clifford Baxter, a VICE-CHAIRMAN of Enron until his resignation in May 2001, was found shot dead. He had been one of the first to see the problems at Enron and had heated arguments about the accounting for off-balance-sheet financing, which he found unacceptable. Herbert Weinokur and Robert Jaedicke, OUTSIDE DIRECTORS and members of the Enron AUDIT COMMITTEE, claimed that the board was either not informed or was deceived about deals involving the SPEs.

Early in 2002, David Duncan, the former lead partner on Enron's audit, who had allegedly shredded Enron files and been fired by Andersen, co-operated with the Justice Department's criminal indictment. He became a whistle-blower, pleading guilty to charges that he did "knowingly, intentionally and corruptly persuade and attempt to persuade Andersen partners and employees to shred documents".

Why did it happen?
There are three principal reasons:

- Enron switched strategy from energy supplier to energy trader, effectively becoming a financial institution with an increased risk profile.

- Enron's financial strategy hid corporate debt and exaggerated performance.
- US accounting standards permitted the off-balance-sheet treatment of the SPES.

What are the implications?
There are implications in four areas:

E

- CORPORATE GOVERNANCE in the United States, including the roles of the CEO and board of directors and the issue of DUALITY; the independence of outside, NON-EXECUTIVE DIRECTORS; the functions and membership of the audit committee; and the oversight role of institutional SHAREHOLDERS.
- Regulation in American financial markets, including the regulation of industrial companies with financial trading arms like Enron; the responsibilities of the independent credit rating agencies; the regulation of American pension funds; and the effect on the world's capital markets.
- Accounting standards, particularly accounting for off-balance-sheet SPES; the regulation of the American accounting profession; and the convergence of American GAAP with International accounting standards.
- Auditing, including auditor independence; auditors' right to undertake non-audit work for audit clients; the rotation of audit partners; audit firms or government involvement in audit; the need for a cooling-off period before an auditor joins the staff of a client company.

Some people outside the United States have thought that the Enron debacle was a uniquely American phenomenon, reflecting its corporate regulation, accounting standards and legal situation. But subsequent collapses and downward revisions of past results by companies in other parts of the world suggest that the Enron lessons have wider relevance. Certainly, the Enron experience has changed the risk and reward of auditing. It has also reduced the big five global accounting firms to four, with the demise of Andersen.

AFTER THE EVENT:

The company appeared not merely to gently grill its accounts – they were seemingly roasted to a cinder. Enron, it seems, was almost a virtual company, with virtual profits.

John Stittle, chartered secretary, 2002

E

A core of Enron executives deceived everyone. Enron Corporation, formerly one of the world's largest and most profitable companies in the United States, imploded with revelations of improper accounting practices, and alleged inadequate audits, mismanagement, and the failure of the board of directors to perform its fiduciary duty to shareholders.
CalPERS, a major pension fund, reporting how much it had lost in the Enron collapse and why

My proposals to safeguard shareholders from another Enron collapse centre on three core principles of providing better information to investors, making corporate officers more accountable and developing a stronger, more independent audit system.

George W. Bush, American president, 2002

Too many elements of the system (of regulating auditors) are not trustworthy today. They have failed us because of self-dealing and self-interest. Auditors must be banned from consulting on how to structure transactions, such as the kinds of special purpose entities that Enron engaged in ... (which) only serve to help management get around the rules.

Arthur Levitt, former chairman, Securities and Exchange Commission

---

ERISA

See EMPLOYEE RETIREMENT INCOME SECURITY ACT.

ESOP

See EMPLOYEE SHARE OWNERSHIP PLAN.

Ethical funds

Investment funds, such as mutual and unit trusts, run by INSTI-TUTIONAL INVESTORS, dedicated to investing in companies that meet certain ethical criteria, such as providing environmental benefits or not trading in weapons, polluting processes or deforestation. Thus far such funds wield little power, other than raising awareness.

E

Ethics

As markets and business have become global and more open to international scrutiny, more attention has been paid to corporate ethics. Well-publicised financial scandals around the world, such as ENRON, HIH INSURANCE and MAXWELL, have focused the spotlight on CORPORATE SOCIAL RESPONSIBILITY. Environmental tragedies, such as Union Carbide's plant explosion in Bhopal, which killed and maimed many people in India, or the Exxon Valdez oil spill in Alaska, sharpened the focus. Increasingly, public opinion demands that boards of directors exercise their considerable powers for good or harm with responsibility and in the interests of the many who can be affected, rather than solely in the interests of SHAREHOLDERS and the short-term bottom line. Understandably, some directors feel that their job is to ensure that the company is profitable, while obeying the law, and that if a society wants companies to behave in a specific way it must pass legislation to that effect. But ultimately a directorship is a position of trust, demanding absolute integrity, including the ability to make moral judgments, recognising the broader and longer-term societal interests that can be affected by board decisions, and distinguishing the company's interests from personal interests.

The European Union has rejected a regulatory approach to corporate social responsibility, emphasising instead its voluntary nature. But it does encourage companies to include social and environmental information in their annual reports through a set of voluntary guidelines. France is the first European country to require companies to disclose details of their social responsibility practices. From 2004, all French LISTED COMPA-NIES will have to report on their adherence to the International Labour Organisation's core principles on energy, the environment and social impact. (See also SUSTAINABLE DEVELOPMENT.)

E

Four years of violence swept through the Krasnoyarsk aluminium smelting company in Siberia as gangsters, fraud and death threats were used to gain control. When the smoke cleared dozens of executives, bankers and mob bosses were dead.

Russian Institute of Directors, www.rid.ru

Our code of ethics rests on a conceptual framework of fundamental principles and an analysis of threats and safeguards, rather than an ever-increasing number of rules that inevitably fail to cover every eventuality.

Neil Learner, chairman, ICAEW Ethics Group

European Corporate Governance Institute

The European Corporate Governance Institute (ECGI) aims to improve governance through fostering independent scientific research and related activities. Formerly the European Corporate Governance Network, it has academic, corporate and ordinary members. The ECGI board has 11 members – six academics and five non-academics – and is based in Brussels.

www.ecgi.org

Executive director

A member of the board who is also employed by the company in a management capacity. As executives, such directors are employees of the company, with rights and duties under employment law. As directors, however, they are responsible like all other directors under company law, as the law makes no distinction between types of director. One of the major challenges to an executive director is to be able to separate the two roles: on the one hand to perform as a member of senior management running the enterprise, and on the other to be a member of the board, jointly responsible with the other directors to see that it is being run well and in the right direction.

Executive supervision

The monitoring of management performance throughout the company, one of the principal elements of the board's activities. With a UNITARY BOARD, particularly if the EXECUTIVE DIRECTORS are in the majority or dominate board proceedings, objective monitoring and evaluation of executive performance may be diluted. Strong chairmanship of the board is then needed. With the supervisory or TWO-TIER BOARD structure, this responsibility falls to the upper SUPERVISORY BOARD. However, many unitary boards devote the greater part of their time and effort to this function, with their board papers mainly reporting financial results and recent operating data. Such a concentration on the compliance and CONFORMANCE ROLE of the board, consequently, allows less time for its PERFORMANCE ROLE and responsibilities.

One of the problems of a board dominated by executive directors is that they are marking their own examination papers.
Lord Caldecote, when chairman of the Delta Group; had he been commenting today, he might have added "and worse, many of them are awarding themselves the prizes"

Family company

A company in which members of a family exercise control, either because a majority of the voting shares are held by family members or because family interests exercise sufficient influence over affairs to control board membership. Many family companies are CLOSELY HELD COMPANIES. But a PUBLIC COMPANY can also be a family company: Coca-Cola, Ford Motor Company, Hewlett-Packard, Microsoft and Wal-Mart are examples.

Family director

A director of a company in which the controlling shares are held within a family. A family company is frequently a CLOSELY HELD COMPANY during the lifetime of the founder. On succession, however, differences can arise. Some shares may pass to members of the family who are no longer involved in management, although they remain NON-EXECUTIVE DIREC-TORS. They want profits and dividends. They are concerned about expensive benefits available to the EXECUTIVE DIREC-TORS. Another conflict can arise if the second and third generations of the family expect to provide the senior management, whereas the company really needs to recruit professional management.

We may not do much good, but at least we don't do any harm.
Fin Guinness, commenting on the role of the family directors in Guinness, in *Requiem for a Family Business*, 1997

FASB

See FINANCIAL ACCOUNTING STANDARDS BOARD.

Fat cat

The label "fat cat" has been applied to directors in both the United States and the UK whose DIRECTORS' REMUNERATION appears to be excessive for their contribution to the company. GOLDEN HANDCUFFS, GOLDEN HANDSHAKES, GOLDEN HELLOS, GOLDEN PARACHUTES and SHARE OPTIONS have all been used as evidence of excessive rewards, particularly when seen as rewarding failure.

F

Fiduciary duty

Directors in most jurisdictions are expected to act with honesty, integrity and candour towards their company, in particular towards the interests of its SHAREHOLDERS. This fiduciary duty is to the company as a whole, to both majority and minority shareholders, should they exist. This can be difficult for a NOMINEE DIRECTOR who has been elected to safeguard the interest of the nominating shareholder, or where a dominant parent company exercises power over its subsidiary even though there are minority outside shareholders. Common law based on the Commonwealth (in Australia, Canada, Hong Kong, India, New Zealand, Singapore, South Africa and so on) allows directors to determine the best interests of the whole company, subject to the right of appeal to the courts. Directors of companies incorporated in the United States owe specific fiduciary duties to any minority shareholders. In other words, the primary duty of a director is to act honestly in good faith, giving all shareholders equal, sufficient and accurate INFORMATION on all issues affecting their interests. The underlying (and universal) principle is that directors should not treat a company as though it exists for their personal benefit. (See also DUTY OF CARE.)

   The seven principles of public life, drawn up by Lord Nolan, chairing a committee of the great and the good, to guide the British government, are highly appropriate to directors fulfilling their fiduciary duty. Nolan's principles were:

- selflessness – holders of public office should serve the public interest, not seek gains for their friends;
- integrity – they should not place themselves under financial obligation to outsiders who might influence their duties;
- objectivity – they should award public appointments and contracts on merit;
- ACCOUNTABILITY – they should submit themselves to the appropriate scrutiny;
- openness – they should give reasons for their decisions;
- honesty – they should declare conflicts of interest;
- leadership – they should support these principles by personal example.

Figurehead

One of the roles a director can play (see PERFORMANCE ROLES.)

Filibustering

See MEETING MANIPULATION.

The current system of disclosure is designed to avoid liability not to inform anybody. There is no true number in accounting, and if there were auditors would be the last people to find it.
Harvey Pitt, when chairman of the SEC

Financial Accounting Standards Board

The organisation that sets GENERALLY ACCEPTED ACCOUNT-ING PRINCIPLES (GAAP) in the United States. After the ENRON debacle, the Financial Accounting Standards Board (FASB) was attacked for insisting on standards that are too detailed, allowing companies to stay within the rules but evade the spirit of accounting principles, which is to provide a true and fair view.

www.fasb.org

Financial analysts

See INVESTMENT ANALYST.

Financial engineering

See COOKING THE BOOKS.

F

Financial Services Authority

The overall REGULATOR for the financial services industry in the UK. The Financial Services Authority (FSA) claims to operate through a risk-based rather than a rules-based approach. In 2000, it took over responsibility for listing companies from the London Stock Exchange and publishes the LISTING RULES, originally called the *Yellow Book* – although the new rulebook has a purple binder.

www.fsa.gov.uk

Financial Reporting Council

A UK body which is dedicated to good financial reporting, and oversees the work of the ACCOUNTING STANDARDS BOARD and the Financial Reporting Review Panel.

Fund management

In managing their mutual funds, unit trusts and other investment products, INSTITUTIONAL INVESTORS have the potential to play a significant role in CORPORATE GOVERNANCE. Some commentators (the HAMPEL REPORT, for example) have called on them to exercise their VOTING RIGHTS, acting as mediator on behalf of all the SHAREHOLDERS, policing recalcitrant boards, attacking excessive DIRECTORS' REMUNERATION when necessary and generally supporting the creation of

SHAREHOLDER VALUE. Others are less sure that institutional investors should be involved in such SHAREHOLDER ACTIVISM, pointing out that fund managers do not form a homogeneous group. At one extreme are funds, which have a purely short-term orientation; at the other are RELATIONSHIP INVESTORS, who often seek a seat on the board. Most fund managers around the world fall between these extremes.

F

The issues of power and accountability were raised at the outset in relation to corporate boards. They will increasingly be raised in the context of the growing power and relative lack of accountability of institutional investors. Their exercise of power over boards will only be seen as legitimate if it is open and reflects the views of those who have entrusted their money to them.

Sir Adrian Cadbury, *Directors' Monthly*, 1998

GAAP

See GENERALLY ACCEPTED ACCOUNTING PRINCIPLES.

Games directors play

Although routinely presented as a serious, analytical and rational process, boardroom behaviour is often intensely political, involving personal rivalries, corporate power plays and networking skills. The games include the following.

- **Alliance building** is a power game played outside the boardroom for ensuring mutual support within. It is closely allied to log rolling.
- **Coalition building** involves canvassing support for an issue informally outside the boardroom so that there is a sufficient consensus when the matter is discussed formally inside the boardroom.
- **Cronyism** is supporting a director's interests even though they may not be in the best interest of the company or its SHAREHOLDERS. For example, a director declares a personal interest in a contract in a tender being discussed by the board; he might even leave the room for the discussion. However, board members support his bid because of their relationship, even though it is not the most worthy. This is sometimes alleged to be the basis of CORPORATE GOVERNANCE in Asia.
- **Deal making** is a classic game usually involving compromise, in which two or more directors reach a behind-the-scenes agreement to achieve a specific outcome in a board decision.
- **Divide and rule** is a dirty game, in which the player sees the chance to set one director against another, or groups of directors against each other. An issue in the financial accounts might be used, for example, to set the EXECUTIVE DIRECTORS, the NON-EXECUTIVE DIRECTORS and the AUDITORS against each other in order to achieve an entirely different personal aim.

- **Empire building** is the misuse of privileged access to INFORMATION, people or other resources to acquire power over organisational territory. The process often involves intrigue, battles and conquests.
- **Half truths** occur if a director, although not deliberately lying, tells only one side of the issue in board deliberations.
- **Hidden agendas** involve directors' pursuit of secret goals to benefit their own empire or further their own career against the interest of the organisation as a whole.
- **Log rolling** occurs when director A agrees, off the record, to support director B's interests, for mutual support when it comes to matters of interest to A.
- **MEETING MANIPULATION**
- **Propaganda** is the dissemination of information to support a cause and is seen more in relationships with shareholders, stockmarkets and financial institutions than in board-level deliberations. The regulatory authorities are likely to act if propaganda becomes excessive or deliberately false.
- **Rival camps** is a game played when there are opposing factions on a board, in which hostilities, spies and double agents can be involved.
- **Scaremongering** emphasises the downside risks in a board decision, casting doubts about the situation, so that the proposal will be turned down.
- **Snowing** involves executive directors deluging an OUTSIDE DIRECTOR seeking further information with masses of data confusing the situation and papering over any cracks.
- **Spinning** is an art form developed at governmental level, which presents a distorted view of a person or a situation, favourable to the interests of the spinner. In corporate governance, spinning can be carried out at the level of the board, the shareholders or the media.
- **Sponsorship** is support by a powerful director for another, usually for their joint benefit.
- **Suboptimisation** occurs when a director supports a part of the organisation to the detriment of the company as a

whole. Some executive directors suffer from tunnel vision because they are too closely involved with a functional department or a subsidiary company, and from short-sighted myopia because they will be personally affected by the outcome. An independent evaluation of senior management performance by outside directors can help to overcome such problems.

◪ **Window dressing** produces a fine external show of sound corporate governance principles while covering up failures. Window dressing can also involve showing financial results in the best possible light while hiding weaknesses.

Directors with integrity and strong chairmanship will reduce the opportunities for game playing.

"In my experience ..." is one of the most over-used phrases in board-level discussions. The question that should always be asked is whether that experience is relevant to the subject in hand.

As they say in board meetings, "Trust me on this".
Peanuts

GENERAL ELECTRIC

General Electric (GE) was one of America's largest and most successful groups, operating in the electrical appliance, power generation, aircraft engine and financial sectors. Under Jack Welch's leadership, it became an icon for business success. After his retirement, concerns were expressed about the accounting methods used by the group's financial arm. His own retirement benefits, including the use of the company's plane, also came under scrutiny, not because of information disclosed in SEC filings, but through information supplied by his wife in divorce proceedings.

Jeffrey Immelt, Welch's successor, proposed changes to GE's CORPORATE GOVERNANCE designed to strengthen the board's oversight of management and to serve the long-term interests of

SHAREHOLDERS, employees and other STAKEHOLDERS. He claimed that these changes would go beyond the SARBANES-OXLEY ACT and the NEW YORK STOCK EXCHANGE LISTING RULES. DISCLOSURE and transparency would be improved. Two-thirds of the directors would be genuinely independent. The CHAIRMAN of the COMPENSATION COMMITTEE would serve as presiding director and chair at least three meetings each year of the non-employee (or outside) directors. In December each year the CEO would discuss future strategic, risk and integrity issues with the board, which would schedule discussions on these topics over the year. Each director would visit two GE plants a year without members of senior management present. OUTSIDE DIRECTORS who are CEOs should not serve on more than two other PUBLIC COMPANY boards, and other directors should not serve on more than four. Two outside directors stepped down because the aggregate business that their firms did with GE accounted for more than 1% of their revenue. In 2003, the GE board had 17 directors, 11 of them independent.

www.ge.com

It is incontrovertibly clear that long-standing deficiencies in the system we employ to produce quality audits of financial statements have caused a serious threat to the efficacy of our capital markets: we're experiencing a significant loss of investor confidence in public companies, their audited financial statements and the accounting profession.
Harvey Pitt, when chairman of the SEC, 2002

Generally accepted accounting principles

There are essentially two sets of accounting standards recognised around the world: American generally accepted accounting principles (GAAPS) and international GAAPS. The American GAAPS provide a detailed, legally oriented set of rules for dealing with various accounting situations, such as leases, depreciation and mergers. Before ENRON, the feeling in the United States was that the American GAAPS provided the better approach to measuring corporate financial performance. Since Enron, there have been

moves towards convergence with INTERNATIONAL AC-
COUNTING STANDARDS, which emphasise basic principles of
accounting rather than detailed and prescriptive rules, and may
be less amenable to different interpretations. (See also FINAN-
CIAL ACCOUNTING STANDARDS BOARD.)

www.fasb.org, www.aicpa.org

Generic strategy

A description of the overall strategic stance of a business. For
example, a company might focus on a specific niche in the
market, adopting a high-price strategy based on products differentiated by brand characteristics, quality or service; or it might
base its strategy on scale, cost-efficiency and market positioning, to compete on price with a low-cost strategy. Further, in assessing strategic options, a company might expand through
internally generated growth and in local, regional or international markets, or adopt a genuinely global strategy locating pro-
curement, manufacturing, assembly, sales and marketing,
servicing, and the provision of finance wherever commercially
and strategically viable. Directors need to share a perception of
their company's generic strategies.

German corporate governance

PUBLIC COMPANIES in Germany have a TWO-TIER BOARD
governance structure: an upper SUPERVISORY BOARD (the Auf-
sichtsrat) and an executive board or committee (the Vorstand).
The supervisory board requires the executive board to present
its proposals and plans to it for comment and approval, then
reviews and assesses subsequent managerial performance. The
power of the supervisory board lies in its ability to appoint and
remove executives from the executive committee. In Germany,
the CO-DETERMINATION process requires, in large organisations, a close relationship between capital and labour. Consequently, supervisory boards in Germany have equal numbers
of representatives of SHAREHOLDERS and of employees.

Common membership of supervisory and executive boards is not permitted. In 2002, the German Corporate Governance Commission launched a code of best practice (Kodex), which provided supervisory boards with more powers over management and external AUDIT, required details of DIRECTORS' REMUNERATION (including the criteria for performance-based rewards) and called for more timely information for investors. No more than two former executives may join the supervisory board at any time. Although they are technically voluntary, some of the provisions have been enshrined in company law. From 2003, German companies must issue an annual statement, published online, showing whether they have complied with the code and explaining any discrepancies. A "balance sheet police force" is also planned, similar to the PUBLIC COMPANIES OVERSIGHT BOARD under the SARBANES-OXLEY ACT.

Global Corporate Governance Forum

An initiative of the World Bank and the Organisation for Economic Co-operation and Development (OECD) to promote improved CORPORATE GOVERNANCE. The forum arranges round-table discussions and promotes the OECD PRINCIPLES of corporate governance.

www.gcgf.org

Global Reporting Initiative

An international multi-stakeholder effort to create a common framework for voluntary reporting of the economic, environmental and social impact of organisations' activities. The mission of the Global Reporting Initiative (GRI) is to enhance the comparability and credibility of sustainability reporting practices worldwide. It incorporates the active participation of businesses and accountancy, human rights, environmental, labour and governmental organisations. (See also SUSTAINABLE DEVELOPMENT.)

Global shares

Global shares were invented by the New York Stock Exchange to facilitate the Daimler/Chrysler "merger" in 1998. The advantage of global shares over AMERICAN DEPOSITARY RECEIPTS is that they can be traded electronically around the world in many markets and multiple currencies. The Daimler/Chrysler shares began trading on 21 exchanges in eight countries.

Global shares enable virtually seamless cross-border trading, allowing non-US companies to increase liquidity and pricing efficiency in the US market while permitting US investors access to home market shares on the same terms as local investors.
New York Stock Exchange, July 2002

G

Golden handcuffs

A term in an executive DIRECTOR'S CONTRACT which binds him to the company for a given period for a substantial reward.

Golden handshake

A bountiful reward given to a director on the termination of his contract, often negotiated when the contract is first signed. Such rewards are sometimes criticised because the extent of the handshake bears no relation to the contribution the director has made to the company – sometimes the reverse. (See also DIRECTORS' CONTRACTS and DIRECTORS' REMUNERATION.)

Golden hello

A one-off payment made to a director as an incentive to join a company, typically recognising some of the benefits forgone by leaving the previous company and acknowledging the additional costs and risk involved in the move.

Golden parachute

A device written into some executive DIRECTORS' CONTRACTS or offered on a potential takeover which enables them to float away from the company with exorbitant severance pay.

Golden share

A share in a company that gives overall voting power in that company to its owner, usually if something specific, such as a takeover bid, occurs. A typical example is a public-sector business, such as a power, transport or telecommunications company, which is privatised. The government holds the golden share so that it can prevent control passing to a foreign corporation. As business becomes more global, the use of golden shares is decreasing. Moreover, in 2002 the European Court of Justice issued a ruling limiting governments' use of golden shares on the grounds that such shares acted as a restriction on the MARKET FOR CONTROL. The British government's golden share in BAA, the UK airports operator, was declared illegal by the European Court in 2003.

Governing body

All CORPORATE ENTITIES need to be governed, and the governing body fulfils that need. In the case of a JOINT STOCK LIMITED LIABILITY COMPANY, the governing body is typically the board of directors. In other corporate entities, it may be called the council, the senate, the executive committee, even the governing body. Most of the ideas and insights in this book can be applied to such bodies.

Effective corporate governance is essential for an economy based on investment and production, in much the same way that effective governance is essential for the operation of a successful democracy.
Ann Robinson, inaugural lecture Bournemouth University, 2001

Governing director

A phrase used mainly in Australia to describe a director with dominant powers in a PRIVATE COMPANY. Although legislation requires such companies to have two directors, the statutes do not prevent companies framing their ARTICLES OF ASSOCIATION to give virtually all powers to one person: the governing director.

Greenmail

G

Arbitrageurs who buy shares on the possibility of a takeover bid, with the intention of bidding up the price to sell at a profit, or acquiring a sufficient stake to block the bidder and force one side or the other to buy the shares at a premium to obtain control, are indulging in greenmail.

Greenbury Report

See DIRECTORS' REMUNERATION.

GUINNESS

In 1985 Guinness, a brewer, set its sights on Distillers, owner of internationally known brands of whisky. Distillers received another hostile bid from Argyll, a retail chain. Under the leadership of Ernest Saunders, who was CHAIRMAN and CEO, Guinness made a counter bid with a £2.6 billion share and cash offer, and was eventually successful. Later it emerged that the market for Guinness shares had been rigged, with the help of Ivan Boesky, a New York arbitrageur. Three other directors were implicated in the share support scheme. All served time in jail, although Saunders was released early when he was diagnosed as having Alzheimer's disease, from which he later made a remarkable recovery. Subsequently, the European Court of Justice ruled that the convictions were unfair, but the English Court of Appeal refused to quash their convictions.

Hampel Report

This 1998 report from the Committee on Corporate Governance, chaired by Sir Ronnie Hampel, was a successor to the British CADBURY and Greenbury reports. It offered a set of "principles of CORPORATE GOVERNANCE", reflecting current conventional wisdom on corporate governance with three prevailing themes.

- That good corporate governance needs broad principles not prescriptive rules. Compliance with sound governance practices, such as the separation of board chairmanship from chief executive, should be flexible and relevant to each company's individual circumstances and not reduced to what the report calls a "box-ticking" exercise. Self-regulation is the preferred approach; no more company legislation is needed.
- That the board is accountable to the company's SHAREHOLDERS. There is no case for redefining directors' responsibilities to other STAKEHOLDER groups.
- That the UNITARY BOARD is totally accepted in the UK. There is no interest in other governance structures or processes such as TWO-TIER BOARDS.

Predictably, perhaps, a committee comprised predominantly of directors of major PUBLIC COMPANIES and their professional advisers did not criticise contemporary corporate governance, nor did it advocate any measures which would further limit directors' power to make unfettered decisions or widen the scope of their ACCOUNTABILITY. Shortly after the report was published, the British government announced a new fundamental review of UK company law.

In corporate governance, we shall work for less regulation and against the idea of a permanent standing committee (on corporate governance), which would most likely look for ways of interfering with and regulating corporate activity.

Tim Melville-Ross, formerly secretary-general, Institute of Directors, London, 1997

Harmonisation of company law

Several jurisdictions have tried to harmonise their company laws. The European Union has had a company law harmonisation programme for many years, although that has largely been overtaken by social legislation affecting CORPORATE GOVERNANCE issues (see WORKER DIRECTOR). Australia and Canada have also developed business acts at the federal level, provoking adverse reactions from the states and provinces involved, which feared a loss of autonomy and tax revenue. In the United States, companies can only be incorporated in individual states; there is no federal companies legislation, only federal securities legislation. This is why companies may incorporate in states such as Delaware, which have relatively liberal company laws.

H

Corporations are truly getting to the same place as Church and nation state before them, where the position of the leader rather than the institution becomes paramount. This is the condition that precedes loss of legitimacy and collapse.
Robert Monks, *The New Global Investors*, www.ragm.com

Helicopter vision

An essential requirement for every director: the ability to perceive issues at different levels of abstraction. When a helicopter is on the ground the pilot can see every blade of grass, but he cannot see very far. As the helicopter rises, more and more comes into the pilot's vision but in less and less detail. At a considerable height it is possible to see to the distant horizon and scan all the ground in between; but the detail of individual elements has now been lost.

So it is with directors' thinking. Helicopter vision involves being able to think, for example, at the level of the personalities involved in a situation, at the level of departments, STRATEGIC BUSINESS UNITS or subsidiaries, or the company as a whole, or the industry, internationally or even globally. Some people, perhaps because of their professional training or earlier experience, think only at a single level. They do not make good directors. Those who can perceive issues at different levels have board potential.

But the greatest challenge to a director is not just to have helicopter vision, since many people can achieve this with experience. The difficult part is to decide which level is appropriate to the matter at hand. Far too many decisions are made at an inappropriate level. Perhaps a decision is treated as an operational matter, failing to recognise the managerial or strategic aspects; or the reverse, making a strategic decision, failing to recognise the operational implications.

H

Hidden agendas

See GAMES DIRECTORS PLAY.

Higgs Report

Yet another report on CORPORATE GOVERNANCE, sponsored by the British government and published in 2003, following problems in British companies such as Cable & Wireless and MARCONI and reflecting concerns about American companies such as ENRON and WORLDCOM. Written by Derek Higgs, a former corporate financier at Warburg and holder of many directorships, the report reviewed the role and effectiveness of NON-EXECUTIVE DIRECTORS.

The principal recommendations were as follows.

- The roles of CHAIRMAN and chief executive should always be separated.
- No one should chair more than one FTSE 100 company.
- A chief executive should not become chairman of that company.
- At least half of the directors should be independent non-executives.
- A non-executive director should not serve more than two terms of three years.
- A full-time EXECUTIVE DIRECTOR should not take on

more than one additional non-executive directorship and should not be chairman of a FTSE 100 company.

- The non-executive directors should meet at least once a year without the chairman or executive directors present.
- The pool of candidates for non-executive directorships should be broadened.
- Non-executive directors should have more training and their pay should reflect their enlarged role.
- A senior non-executive director should be nominated as a conduit for SHAREHOLDERS to explore any concerns they might have.
- Non-executive directors should be indemnified against legal action.

The proposals supplement the UK COMBINED CODE (see Appendix 1) and maintain the voluntary approach, rather than adopting the American-style regulatory system enshrined in the SARBANES-OXLEY ACT.

More than one in ten chairmen of listed companies hold two chairmanships, while 2% hold more than two. Only 4% of non-executive directors had a formal interview and just 1% had come to the role through advertising.
Higgs Report

Non-executives are typically white males nearing retirement age. We are talking about broadening the view away from the usual suspects ... Almost half of non-executive directors are recruited through personal contacts and friendships. This leads to an over-familiar atmosphere in the boardroom.
Derek Higgs

I don't believe the (Higgs Report) will change the way companies work one iota. If the responsibility for companies is continually pushed on to the non-executives, God help us all.
Donald Gordon, chairman, Liberty International

HIH INSURANCE

HIH Insurance Group was Australia's largest insurer. When it collapsed the £1.9 billion loss left many policyholders and investors bereft. Some lost their homes. A royal commission questioned Ray Williams, the founder and CEO. Observers commented on a tale of "spectacular munificence", saying "it was like the last days of Pompeii". Williams enjoyed a millionaire's lifestyle. His secretary travelled first-class. A corporate adviser was given round-the-world air tickets for himself, his wife, four children and a nanny to compensate for working over Christmas. Rodney Adler, a director, whose FAI insurance company HIH had been taken over for more than £200m in 1998, received a £2.3m termination payment and a £350,000 a year consultancy fee. Williams, who had donated millions to medical research, claimed that his own life savings were in the company and that he had not sold any shares. The problems, he claimed, were caused by errors of judgment, in particular the failure to undertake a DUE DILIGENCE study on FAI, which had gaping holes in its finances.

Andersen had been the company's AUDITOR and among the evidence given to the Royal Commission was the allegation that there had been no contact between the auditors and the company's actuary. The accountancy regulatory authorities and the liquidator of HIH took note. The liquidator also brought an action against the Australian Prudential (Insurance) Regulation Authority alleging negligence. But the underlying governance question remains: what was the board doing while this saga was going on?

The board's key role is to ensure that corporate management is continuously and effectively striving for above-average performance, taking account of risk. This is not to deny the board's additional role with respect to shareholder protection.
Hilmer Report, *Strictly Boardroom*, 1993

Hilmer Report

A report by Fred Hilmer, published in 1993 by the Sydney Institute with the title *Strictly Boardroom*. (This reflects the film

"Strictly Ballroom", in which competitive ballroom dancing had become so regulated that innovation was stifled.) This, says the report, is what can happen to CORPORATE GOVERNANCE. It advocated an emphasis on the PERFORMANCE ROLES of the board.

IASC

See INTERNATIONAL ACCOUNTING STANDARDS COMMITTEE.

IASB

See INTERNATIONAL ACCOUNTING STANDARDS BOARD.

ICELAND

Malcolm Walker was CHAIRMAN of Iceland, a British frozen food company and the fifth largest food provider in the UK. In late 2000, he cashed in the bulk of his shares in the company for around £13m. Five weeks later the company issued a profits warning that sent the share price crashing. He avoided the immediate aftermath of his action by going on holiday and on his return announced he was retiring. When castigated in the press for selling his shares, Walker claimed that he had done no wrong; his board of directors had full knowledge of the sale and had sanctioned it.

But did they have adequate INFORMATION to make that decision? Were they told of the daily figures, which were, no doubt, already pointing to the profits warning? Did they question what the impact of the sale might be on investors' confidence and the share price?

Directors do have an obligation to their chairman; he probably nominated them to the board and ensures that their fees are paid. But directors' primary duty is to the company and its SHAREHOLDERS, who have appointed them to look after their interests.

ICGN

See INTERNATIONAL CORPORATE GOVERNANCE NETWORK.

IMA

See INVESTMENT MANAGERS ASSOCIATION.

IMO

See INVESTMENT MANAGEMENT REGULATING AUTHORITY.

Indemnity insurance

The need for personal indemnity by directors against the threat of LITIGATION has become important in many parts of the world. Litigation brought by SHAREHOLDERS and others alleging misfeasance, breach of duty, negligence or other actions in damages, against companies, their boards, their AUDITORS and, particularly, against individual named directors, has been increasing. The predilection towards litigation began in the United States but it has spread. Auditors and directors in Australia, the UK and other countries are now increasingly subject to lawsuits that may involve huge claims for damages. Nowadays it is sensible for directors to ensure that they are adequately covered by indemnity insurance. Sometimes referred to as D&O (directors and officers) cover, such insurance offers some protection against legal costs and damages awarded. In some jurisdictions, directors have to pay their own premiums since, it is argued, a company may not use its own funds to protect its directors from their own negligence. The ENRON and WORLDCOM CORPORATE GOVERNANCE scandals have made D&O insurance harder to obtain and more expensive throughout the world.

Independent director

An OUTSIDE DIRECTOR or NON-EXECUTIVE DIRECTOR with no interests in the company, other than the directorship, which might affect, or be seen to affect, the exercise of independent judgment. Some REGULATORS, such as the SECURITIES AND

EXCHANGE COMMISSION in the United States, lay down detailed criteria to determine independence. Essentially, however, a director cannot be seen to be independent if he or she (or a connected company) has had significant business dealings with the company (for example, as a supplier, customer, or banker), or if he or she is closely related to the CHAIRMAN or a member of senior management, or is a former executive of the company. Although there may be a good case for people with such connections or experience to be on the board, they cannot be considered to be fully independent, and hence cannot be part of the check-and-balance mechanisms enshrined in the AUDIT COMMITTEE, the NOMINATION COMMITTEE or the REMUNERATION COMMITTEE. Some people serve on many boards and are effectively professional directors. Critics of this development include the UK's Institute of Directors, which has suggested that full-time executives should not hold more than two non-executive directorships and no director should sit on more than six boards.

www.independentdirector.co.uk

I think the whole idea of independence is bunkum – and dangerous too. It leads to a "them" and "us" approach with the independent directors feeling they carry the can for the executives and the executives leaving governance to part-timers.

Prue Leith, cookery expert, business woman and non-executive director

In my view you can't have 20 non-executive jobs and pretend you are doing the job properly. My personal limit is three non-executive directorships, and I will not stay on the board for more than six years. I also think that the chairman shouldn't be there for too long. My limit is six years. You avoid the risk of excessive power.

Sir John Collins, chairman, Dixons

The division of responsibility between directors, auditor and senior management is not sufficiently clear. The focus is almost entirely on defining the responsibilities of directors. Yet the commercial reality of the matter is that, in these days of conglomerates and perhaps transnational conglomerates at that, the opportunity for non-executive directors to exercise meaningful control over management is as slight as

the ability of ministers to control a vast bureaucracy.
Justice Andrew Rogers in the AWA case, Australia, 1992

Non-executive directors need to act as a "loyal opposition" to management to challenge and check their proposals. However, NEDs can be inhibited from challenging management when management can determine or influence their tenure on the board.
Shann Turnbull, 2002

INDEPENDENT INSURANCE

In June 2001, the board of directors of Independent Insurance were told by advisers PricewaterhouseCoopers that the company was insolvent, its liabilities exceeding its reserves and assets by a quarter of a billion pounds. A provisional liquidator was appointed. Yet only six months earlier Independent Insurance appeared to be worth over £1 billion.

The company had been floated on the stockmarket in 1993 and many analysts favoured the shares. The last published accounts in 2000 showed an operating profit of £40m, although cash outflow was somewhat higher, and KPMG, the AUDITORS, reported that the accounts showed a true and fair view of the state of the company's affairs. Actuaries, hired to review the company's exposure to risk, claimed that the reserves made reasonable allowance for possible claims. Annual returns were duly filed with Companies House and the financial services authorities. Six months later the company had collapsed.

What went wrong? Where were the checks and balances that should have been provided by the board and INDEPENDENT DIRECTORS, the auditors, the actuaries, the analysts and the REGULATORS?

For 14 years Michael Bright had been managing director of Independent Insurance. A man of undoubted entrepreneurial flair, he had many fans in the City of London for his unique way of doing business and the company's "superior underwriting strength". But he was a forceful and charismatic character and, as his reputation grew, he became less and less willing to allow challenges to his authority. One by one his fellow EXECUTIVE DIRECTORS left. Robert McCracken, head of British regional business, left in 1997; Keith Rutter, responsible for liability underwriting, followed in 1998. Alan Clarke, a third member of the triumvirate that had previously kept Bright in check, retired in 1999. Philip Condon, deputy managing director and the other significant executive director, was a close friend of Bright. Garth Ramsay was a non-executive CHAIRMAN of the board and Sir Iain Noble was another non-executive director. KPMG charged £667,000 for its AUDIT, but it gained nearly £1m more for consultancy and other services.

In the first six months of 2001, the financial problems facing Independent Insurance grew. Reinsurance contracts had been negotiated with GE Capital against the possibility of mounting claims. As the financial situation deteriorated, Ramsay replaced Bright. He sought more INFORMATION on the reinsurance contracts and was horrified to learn that, instead of the substantial cover anticipated, Independent was exposed to a potential liability totalling many millions of pounds. For years the company had been putting insufficient cash into its reserves. Risks had been insured at cut prices without board approval. There was now a huge deficit in the company's reserves and, being unable to cap this exposure, it could not raise further equity.

The board had failed to control their dominant chief executive.

I find that it takes a director up to a year before he really understands what is going on in board meetings, and another year before he really contributes anything worthwhile.
Chairman of a large UK company

Induction programme

An induction programme can provide a new director with valuable information and training. Although often said to be "promoted" to the board for their successful executive performance, many EXECUTIVE DIRECTORS have little knowledge and experience of board-level work. Conversely, a NON-EXECUTIVE

DIRECTOR may have little knowledge of the company and its industry. The purpose of a directors' induction programme is to speed up the time by which a director can really contribute to the board. (See the induction checklist for new directors in Appendix 4.)

The best teachers of directors are board chairmen.
David Leighton, 2002

Industry analysis

STRATEGY FORMULATION has to be competitor- and customer-based and is often global in context. For many directors industry analysis is the starting point for thinking about CORPORATE STRATEGY. Michael Porter, a professor at Harvard Business School, has outlined five driving forces of competitive analysis (see Figure 11).

Taking an industry perspective has greatly changed the strategic battlefield for many boards. No longer are they constrained by thinking primarily about their own products and services and how to market them. Now they focus on the needs of customers and potential customers. They review the strategies being

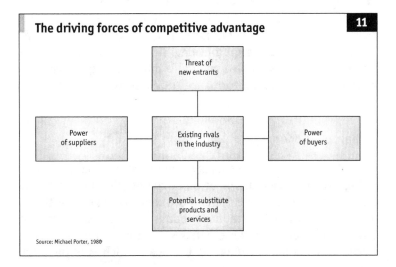

The driving forces of competitive advantage   11

Threat of new entrants

Power of suppliers

Existing rivals in the industry

Power of buyers

Potential substitute products and services

Source: Michael Porter, 1980

pursued by their competitors. They identify potential new competitors and think about what barriers there are to entry into the field. They consider what developments, perhaps in technology, delivery systems or new products, might cause customers to change their allegiance. In other words, many directors are now thinking strategically before they get down to approving plans for their own company.

One of the difficulties of industry analysis is actually determining the boundaries of the industry. Industries overlap: telecommunications and computers, publishing and the internet, retail banking and financial services. STRATEGIC ALLIANCES increasingly cross the frontiers of traditional industries. Potential competitors may come from what appeared to be a non-competing industry.

Information

Directors have the right to the information they feel is necessary for them to fulfil their responsibilities as directors. Some CHAIRMEN make a great effort to ensure that the directors of the company are provided with the information they need, both through formal board papers, board and individual briefings and through INDUCTION PROGRAMMES. But in some companies directors are provided with no more than standard packs for BOARD MEETINGS, with inadequate information, much of which is tabled during the meeting. Computer-based information systems are available that enable directors to gain access to relevant director-level information. (See also WAR ROOM.)

Initial public offering

The sale of newly issued shares by an investment bank, usually to big investing institutions or other contacts, on behalf of the issuing company. Before the end of fixed trading commissions and deregulation, investment banks offered independent advice. Subsequently, these banks sold initial public offerings (IPOS) at a hefty percentage of the deal, which was lucrative and led to SPINNING. This was brought to a halt by the stock-market collapse of 2000–02. (See also INVESTMENT ANALYST.)

I don't need to raise any capital,
so why should I care about corporate governance?
Director of a Russian company, 2002

Inside information

Confidential information about a company's affairs known only to those inside the company. Using such information to buy shares to make a profit or sell shares to prevent a loss is INSIDER DEALING.

Insider dealing

Trading in a LISTED COMPANY's shares on the basis of privileged, share-price sensitive INSIDE INFORMATION would be a breach of a director's FIDUCIARY DUTY. It is also illegal in most countries. Japan, Hong Kong and Germany were among the last countries to make insider dealing a criminal offence, although so far there have been few successful prosecutions. The problem is often that it is difficult to prove that a particular transaction was made as a result of inside information. The United States has the most severe penalties for insider dealing.

The argument against the practice, whether buying shares in the secret knowledge of events that would drive the price up, or selling shares to avoid a loss given secret intelligence on events that would cause the price to fall, is not so much that it is unfair, or because it involves a misuse of information, but because insider dealing destroys the credibility and the integrity of the market. Directors have to be particularly careful not to trade in their company's shares when they are possession of inside information, such as the company results just before publication and before the stockmarket has that information. The COMPANY SECRETARY should inform directors when the window of opportunity for trading in the company's shares is open and, more importantly, when it is closed.

> *Private information is practically the source for*
> *every large modern fortune.*
> Oscar Wilde, *The Ideal Husband*

> *I think public comment can be a very dangerous way of working for an*
> *institutional shareholder. We are here to enhance the value of people's*
> *money. We wouldn't in any way want to cause problems by making*
> *comments in public.*
> Lawrence Burr, managing director, NSW State Superannuation Investment and
> Management Corporation, Australia, *Company Director*, 1993

Institutional investor

A financial institution with shareholdings in listed companies. Institutional investors include pension funds, investment trusts, mutual funds (or unit trusts), life and other insurance companies, and banks running investment portfolios for clients. The proportion of shares held by institutional investors has been increasing throughout the world. In the UK it is now well over 50%. Often institutional investors show little interest in the CORPORATE GOVERNANCE of the companies in which they invest, preferring to take a short-term perspective and VOTING WITH THEIR FEET if they are dissatisfied with a company's performance. Some fund managers, however, have taken a stand in specific cases and voted their shares accordingly. Some institutions have been prominent in these developments, including recently CALPERS and the UK-based Hermes Fund. (See also RELATIONSHIP INVESTING.)

www.calpers.com, www.hermes.co.uk

> *Three-quarters of institutional investors in Europe and America are*
> *prepared to pay a premium between 12% and 14% for stocks that*
> *demonstrate good corporate governance.*
> McKinsey study, 2002

The most important question raised by the emergence of the pension funds, and other institutional investors, as the main suppliers of capital and the majority owners of the large business, is their role and function in the economy. Their emergence makes obsolete all traditional ways of managing and controlling large business. It forces us to think through and redefine the governance of companies.

Peter Drucker, *Post-Capitalist Society*, 1993

Interlocking directorship

A term for directors that sit on each other's boards, sometimes called a cross-directorship. In certain circumstances, such as in a STRATEGIC ALLIANCE, there can be benefits in cross-directorships. But generally the practice is suspect because of the often undisclosed concentration of power. Many studies in the UK and the United States have analysed the structure of cross-directorships, which can involve complex networks of linkages as well as direct links with A on B's board and B on A's board. (See also JAPANESE CORPORATE GOVERNANCE.)

International accounting standards

Published financial statements meeting international standards set by the INTERNATIONAL ACCOUNTING STANDARDS BOARD. International accounting standards (IAS) are recognised for cross-border reporting in 52 countries, although most still require local standards for local companies. They will become mandatory throughout the European Union by 2005 for publicly traded companies, removing barriers to cross-border trading in securities by ensuring that financial statements throughout the Union are compatible and transparent. (See also GENERALLY ACCEPTED ACCOUNTING PRINCIPLES.)

www.pwcglobal.com, www.dti.gov.uk/consultations, www.icaew.co.uk

International Accounting Standards Board

Founded in 1973 as the International Accounting Standards Committee, the International Accounting Standards Board (IASB) was created in 2001 as an independent body responsible for setting international financial reporting standards. Over 150 accounting bodies from over 100 countries are members. The national standard-setting bodies in eight countries – Australia, Canada, France, Germany, Japan, New Zealand, the UK and the USA – have an IASB member resident in their jurisdiction. The aim of the IASB is to create a single set of high-quality, understandable and enforceable global accounting standards, which will provide transparent and comparable information.

www.iasb.org.uk

International Corporate Governance Network

In 1995 a number of parties interested in CORPORATE GOVERNANCE formed the International Corporate Governance Network (ICGN) to co-ordinate their efforts. These included CALPERS and the Council of Institutional Investors in the United States, the ASSOCIATION OF BRITISH INSURERS and NATIONAL ASSOCIATION OF PENSION FUNDS in the UK, the Corporate Governance Forum of the Centre for European Policy Studies and others. Many leading pension funds and INSTITUTIONAL INVESTORS have since joined. An estimated $10 trillion is under investment by member organisations. The ICGN secretariat is based in London.

www.icgn.org

Attacking the barriers to cross-border voting is a powerful new demand from US institutions to vote shares worldwide.
Stephen Davis, *Global Proxy Watch*, 1997

International Organisation of Securities Commissions

A voluntary organisation of financial REGULATORS from over 50 countries, whose members regulate the vast majority of securities traded worldwide. Regular meetings are held to cooperate, exchange information, unite standard-setting efforts and provide mutual assistance to promote the integrity of markets. So the regulation of financial markets and the monitoring of abnormal trading in shares is now global. It is increasingly difficult for INSIDER TRADERS to bury dealings through transactions in overseas markets. The International Organisation of Securities Commissions (IOSCO) is based in Madrid, Spain, and looks to the INTERNATIONAL ACCOUNTING STANDARDS BOARD to provide acceptable international accounting and financial reporting standards.

www.iosco.org

This stock (Infospace Inc) is a powder keg, given how aggressive we were on it earlier in the year, and given the bad smell comments that so many institutions are now bringing up.
Henry Blodget, financial analyst at Merrill Lynch, 2002

Some things never change:
In the last three decades the prestige of security analysis on Wall Street has experienced a brilliant rise and an ignominious fall ... the new era involved the abandonment of the analytical approach (with) facts and figures being manipulated to support the delusions of the period.
Benjamin Graham and David Dodd, Security Analysis, 1934

Investment analyst

A supposedly independent provider of research on LISTED COMPANIES for potential investors. Unfortunately, many investment analysts in both the UK and the United States are employed by financial institutions, which have an interest in promoting the shares of client companies. So their objectivity has been questioned. At worst, analysts have been seen as the puppets of their employing finance house, ramping stocks before they are offered to the public. The problem was exemplified in a 1992 internal staff memorandum from Morgan Stanley: "Our objective is to adopt a policy, fully understood by the entire firm, including the research department, that we do not make negative or controversial comments about a client as a matter of sound business practice." So much for independence. A deal, brokered by Eliot Spitzer, the New York attorney-general in late 2002, which would have required banks to demerge their research divisions into independent companies, and which would have had repercussions on both sides of the Atlantic, failed under pressure from Wall Street. However, some American banks paid substantial penalties after the publication of incriminating evidence of biased research reports. In the UK, Goldman Sachs was also alleged to have given investment advice that was influenced by conflicts of interest between the bank's analysts and its major corporate clients.

Investment Management Regulating Authority

The Investment Management Regulating Authority (IMO) supervises member firms in the UK engaged in investment management and the management and operation of collective investment schemes, and also acts as trustee of regulated collective investment schemes and in-house pension funds. (See also MAXWELL.)

Investment Managers Association

Founded in 2002 from a merger of the Association of Unit Trusts and Investment Funds (AUTIF), a British mutual funds organisation, and the Fund Managers Association (FMA), the Investment Managers Association (IMA) has investment funds of £2 trillion, and intends to seek improvements in CORPORATE GOVERNANCE.

IOSCO

See INTERNATIONAL ORGANISATION OF SECURITIES COMMISSIONS.

IPO

See INITIAL PUBLIC OFFERING.

Japanese corporate governance

Keiretsu are networks of Japanese companies connected through inter-trading, extensive INTERLOCKING DIRECTORSHIPS and CROSS-HOLDINGS. Typically, the network includes a financial institution. CHAIRMEN and senior directors of companies in the *keiretsu* meet regularly and have close, informal relationships. In the past, CORPORATE GOVERNANCE had a STAKEHOLDER, rather than SHAREHOLDER, orientation.

Traditionally, in *keiretsu* companies the board plays a formal, even ritualistic role. Boards are large and almost entirely executive. In effect, the board is the top four or five layers of the management organisation. Promotion to the board, as in the West, is a mark of distinction; but, unlike in the West, interpersonal competition, which has been a feature of life throughout the organisation, continues on the board for promotion to the next level. Senior managers seem often to be younger than their Western counterparts.

However, in recent years, with the worsening economic performance in Japan, the banks at the heart of the *keiretsu* have been weakened and companies have come under increasing pressure, particularly from INSTITUTIONAL INVESTORS abroad, to improve SHAREHOLDER VALUE. More emphasis has, consequently, been placed on shareholders, with board restructuring and director incentives.

The commercial code calls for "representative directors" to be elected by the board. Whereas, from a Western viewpoint, these might be expected to represent the interests of various stakeholders in the firm, their actual role is to represent the company in its dealings with outside parties, such as the government, banks and other companies in the industry. Typically, the representative directors include the chairman, PRESIDENT and other senior directors. The code also calls for the appointment of individuals as full-time statutory AUDITORS. They report to the board on any financial problems or infringements of the company code or the company articles. They can call for information from other directors and company employees and can convene special meetings of the board. These internal board-level auditors, of course, liaise with the external professional auditors.

NON-EXECUTIVE DIRECTORS, in the Western sense, are untypical. A few of the executives might have served with other companies in the *keiretsu* added-value network, and in that sense be able to represent the interests of suppliers or downstream agents; others might have been appointed to the company's ranks on retirement from the *keiretsu*'s bankers or even from among the industry's government REGULATORS (known as a DESCENT FROM HEAVEN). Only recently have independent, OUTSIDE DIRECTORS, been appointed, often under pressure from international sources of capital.

The path to the Japanese board has changed little over the past 40 years. There is only one route and it begins on the first day a new employee, fresh from university, arrives at the corporate offices ... Elevation to the rank of director (is) the supreme reward for competent service, but with little modification in managerial responsibilities ... Eventually many departmental heads are again promoted, becoming simultaneously head of an operating unit and a "managing director". Even the "senior managing directors" are heads of divisions or important staff departments. These are masquerade boards in which managers briefly don the masks of directors.

Aron Viner, "The Coming Revolution in Japan's Board Rooms",
Corporate Governance, Vol. 1, No. 3, July 1993

The Japanese do not see the need for such intervention "from the outside", as they see it. Indeed, they have difficulty in understanding how outside directors function. How can outsiders possibly know enough about the company to make a contribution, they wonder, when they themselves have spent their lives working for it? How can an outsider be sufficiently sensitive to the corporate culture? Worse, might they not damage the harmony of the group by failing to appreciate the subtleties of their relationships?

The social cohesion within Japanese firms is well known, with high levels of unity throughout the organisation, non-adversarial relationships, lifetime employment, enterprise unions, personnel policies emphasising commitment, initiation into the corporate family, decision-making by consensus, cross-functional training, and with promotion based on loyalty and social compatibility as well as performance. But over the past decade, with the Japanese economy facing stagnation, many of these attributes have come under pressure for change. Boards are still often decision-ratifying bodies rather than decision-initiating and decision-taking forums, as in the West. Meetings of the managing directors with the directors in their teams are crucial, as are the informal relationships between the top echelons of the board.

Joint stock limited liability company

A CORPORATE ENTITY formally incorporated under the company law of a given jurisdiction, with a legal existence separate from its owners, whose liability for the company's debts is limited to their shareholding. It is a brilliantly simple, superbly successful mid-19th century idea, and it underpins CORPORATE GOVERNANCE. Without companies there would be no need for directors. However, it is the SHAREHOLDERS' liability that is limited, not the DIRECTORS' LIABILITY.

www.companieshouse.co.uk, www.hemscott.com, www.marketeye.com

All hail astonishing fact,
All hail invention new,
The joint stock company act,
of parliament, sixty two.
And soon or late I always call
for Stock Exchange quotation,
No scheme too great, and none too small
for companification.
Gilbert and Sullivan, *Utopia Ltd*

In the three years 1845–1847, at the height of the railway mania in the UK, 425 new railway companies were incorporated in Britain, with a total proposed capital of over £213 million. This was equal to two-thirds of all exports for 1846. The share capital of the Bank of England at the time was £16.6 million.
Adrian Vaughan, *Railwaymen. Politics and Money*, 1997

Joint venture

See STRATEGIC ALLIANCE.

Judge

One of the roles a director can play (see CONFORMANCE ROLES).

Keiretsu

See JAPANESE CORPORATE GOVERNANCE.

King Report

A South African committee, under the chairmanship of Mervyn King, published a code of corporate practices and conduct in 1994, based on a broad consensus of the South African corporate community. The report includes a "code of ethics for enterprises and all who deal with enterprises".

Lead director

An approach adopted by General Motors (see BOARD CORPOR-
ATE GOVERNANCE POLICIES) and some other major companies, in which an OUTSIDE DIRECTOR is chosen to lead
meetings of the outside directors. Another use of the term can
be found in companies with complex business interests, where
individual directors are given a portfolio of interests on which
they take the lead in board meetings. For example, one director
might lead on new product development, marketing in a specific product group and management of one of the group's international regions.

Legal duties

Directors have two fundamental duties under the company law
of almost all jurisdictions: a FIDUCIARY DUTY to act with
honesty, integrity and candour towards the members of the
company; and a duty to exercise reasonable care, diligence and
skill in their handling of company matters.

Limited liability

See COMPANY LIMITED BY GUARANTEE and JOINT STOCK
LIMITED LIABILITY COMPANY.

Just exactly whose liability is limited in the limited liability company?
A member of the British royal family on taking up a non-executive
directorship. The answer is the shareholders, not the directors.

Limited liability partnership

A new form of CORPORATE ENTITY in the UK. The Partnership
Act of 1890 made partners personally liable for the firm's debts
if the firm became bankrupt, but it did not require partnerships
to publish their accounts. When partnerships were small this

seemed reasonable. But as partnerships grew, particularly in the accountancy profession, the personal exposure of individual partners to their share of the debts of a huge global firm became unacceptable. In a limited liability partnership (LLP), an entity is created that is distinct from its partners, who are known as members. The price of limiting the liability of partners is the requirement to publish accounts that conform to UK accounting standards, just like limited liability companies.

Listed company

A company whose shares are traded on a stock exchange. To be listed on the stock exchange board, the company must satisfy the LISTING RULES of that exchange.

L Listing rules

The regulations that each stock exchange lays down governing the minimum requirements for having a company's shares listed on that market. Typical listing rules include requirements on the contents of prospectuses, on reports and accounts to members, and on matters of board membership, over and above the requirements of the company law in the jurisdiction of incorporation. For example, the London Stock Exchange requires each company's annual report to state whether the requirements of the UK COMBINED CODE have been fulfilled, and if not, why not. The ultimate sanction for failing to meet listing rules is delisting; but since this would disenfranchise public SHAREHOLDERS, which the listing rules are predominantly intended to protect, such sanctions are usually threats used in discussions rather than actions carried out in practice.

Litigation

A growing part of corporate life. AUDIT firms, companies, boards and individual directors are increasingly being exposed to claims for damages in actions brought by SHAREHOLDERS, bankers, customers and others, alleging losses arising through negligence, usually when a company has run into financial difficulties. The former NON-EXECUTIVE DIRECTORS of Equitable Life Assurance Society were sued for £3 billion. Courts will seldom second-guess the business judgment of boards; however, that does not prevent aggrieved parties bringing actions. In the United States, which has become the most litigious country in the world, the threat of legal action sometimes deters people from serving as OUTSIDE DIRECTORS. Even if the INDEMNITY INSURANCE cover is adequate, directors can still face the annoyance and mental suffering of a legal action and the personal embarrassment of media exposure. Some companies, and particularly their AUDITORS, having faced massive claims for damages, can find indemnity insurance prohibitively expensive or even unavailable. (See also ANDERSEN and DEEP-POCKET SYNDROME.)

L

LLP

See LIMITED LIABILITY PARTNERSHIP.

Log-rolling

See GAMES DIRECTORS PLAY.

Low-balling

Using the AUDIT as a loss leader. The practice by AUDITORS of underpricing the audit assignment to win new business in non-audit work.

MARCONI

Marconi grew out of GEC, a company built by Lord Weinstock, who bequeathed a set of solid, if unadventurous, manufacturing businesses, with large reserves of cash. Marconi adopted a different strategy: to invest in high-tech enterprises. Within a few years, all the cash had been spent and the company was over £4 billion in debt. Worse, many of its investments were disasters. In July 2001, the company suspended trading in its shares, warning that profits were likely to halve to around £350m. The company's share price fell and the chief executive, Lord Simpson, met strong opposition to his proposal that executive share options should be repriced to reflect the fall.

Throughout August 2001 the company refused to comment on rumours that things were much worse. No advice was given to investors, the stock exchange or the FINANCIAL SERVICES AUTHORITY. Then in September 2001 the scale of the disaster became clear, when a loss of £327m for the three months to June was announced. Various operating explanations were forthcoming: the downturn in the high-tech market was global; the internal control systems had failed to identify financial problems fast enough; the corporate centre was out of touch with its struggling divisions. The opinion that this was a case of poor business judgment, not of CORPORATE GOVERNANCE, smacks of complacency.

Where was the board during this developing debacle? The case raises questions far beyond strategic and operational mismanagement. The issues go to the heart of the BOARD STRUCTURE and directors' competence. The case for NON-EXECUTIVE DIRECTORS argues that their independence allows them to question senior management and make tough-minded calls for change if necessary. Subsequently, some Marconi non-executive directors claimed that they had questioned both the strategic direction and the financial situation of the company, but had not received the necessary INFORMATION.

But were Marconi's OUTSIDE DIRECTORS truly independent? Lord Simpson of Dunkeld was Marconi's chief executive; he was also a non-executive director of ICI and of the Royal Bank of Scotland, one of Marconi's bankers. Sir Roger Hurn, CHAIRMAN of the Marconi board, was also chairman of Prudential Assurance, a major SHAREHOLDER in Marconi, a non-executive director of ICI and a non-executive of GlaxoSmithKline (as was fellow director Derek Bonham). The non-executive directors included Sir Bill Castell, chief executive of Nycam, formerly finance director at ICI, and Bonham, chairman of Cadbury Schweppes and Imperial Tobacco, who had only recently been appointed to the board. Did their personal connections make this a cosy club, its members too close to ask awkward questions, demand satisfactory answers and insist on decisive action?

A BOARD MEETING was called to face the situation, which one director described as "Britain's greatest industrial disaster for decades". Decisive action was needed. Bonham, as senior non-executive director, took charge. By the end of the meeting both Simpson, the CEO, and Hurn, the chairman, had been replaced.

M

Market for control

The possibility of a hostile takeover bid for the control of a public company supposedly keeps the incumbent directors on their toes. The market for control is well developed in the UK and the United States, but less so in continental Europe and elsewhere in the world. In these countries, legislators believe that aggressive takeovers produce undesirable social costs, and boards are allowed to protect their companies (and themselves) from successful bids by using a POISON PILL.

MAXWELL

Robert Maxwell was born in Slovakia in 1923, grew up in poverty, fought with the Free Czech army and received the British Military Cross. He became an international publishing baron. In the early 1970s, inspectors appointed by the British government led an inquiry into his company Pergamon Press and concluded that he was not "a person who can be relied on to exercise stewardship of a publicly-quoted company". Nevertheless, he subsequently succeeded in building a media empire including two PUBLIC COMPANIES, Maxwell Communication Corporation and Mirror Group Newspapers. Following his death in 1991, in mysterious circumstances at sea, it was alleged that he had used his dominant position as CHAIRMAN of the trustees of the group's pension funds to siphon off funds to support his other interests, and that he had been involved in an illegal scheme to bolster the price of companies in the group. Eventually, the lead companies were declared insolvent and the group collapsed. Investigators estimated that £763m had been plundered from the two public companies and their pension funds to prop up Maxwell's private interests.

There are many lessons for directors in the Maxwell affair. Maxwell's leadership style was dominant: he reserved considerable power to himself and kept his senior executives in the dark. An impressive set of NON-EXECUTIVE DIRECTORS, who added respectability to the public-company boards, were ill informed. Maxwell threatened LITIGATION to prevent criticism of his corporate affairs; many investigative journalists and one doctoral student received writs. The complexity of the group's organisational network, which included PRIVATE COMPANIES incorporated in tax havens with limited DISCLOSURE requirements, made it difficult to obtain a comprehensive overview of group affairs. The failings of the AUDITORS, the trustees of the Maxwell group pension fund and the regulatory bodies were all recognised.

Meeting manipulation

Many BOARD MEETINGS call as much for political acumen and interpersonal skill as for analytical ability and rational argument. There are various devices which the skilful meeting manipulator uses to advantage.

- The management of the AGENDA provides an ideal opportunity: who decides what is discussed and what is not controls the focus of the meeting.

- Lobbying people before the meeting is an obvious trait of a meeting manipulator.

- At the start of the meeting, challenging the MINUTES of the last meeting can be used to reopen discussion of an item that was resolved against your interests last time.

- Quietly taking over the meeting, in other words hijacking the chair, can work.

- Then, should the tenor of the meeting not be to your liking, there are devices to stall or refocus the debate. Talking around the subject, to shift the discussion to favourable issues, is a particular skill of meeting manipulators. Profound irrelevance is their stock in trade. But filibustering to run the discussion out of time will seldom work at board level.

- The put-down involves the skilful introduction of doubt when responding to a proposal before the board, as in: "We discussed this matter before you joined the board and decided against ..." or "The bank would never agree with anything like that ..." These are simple examples; good put-downs can be far more sophisticated.

- Presenting ideas in the context of other people's can be powerful: "I was inclined to believe ... until I heard X, now I wonder whether we should ..." The fact that X was advocating something quite different is irrelevant.

- Summarising the discussion thus far can be used to emphasise favourable points and downplay others: "What the meeting seems to be saying is ..."

- An extension of the summarising device is to predetermine the decision, preferably in Latin, as in: "We seem to have reached the decision, CHAIRMAN, NEM. CON" can be suggested, whether anyone is against or not.

- Where a discussion seems to be flowing against your interests, try a challenge. "On a POINT OF ORDER, chairman" is a call which, if offered with sufficient challenge and conviction, will stop an orator in full flight. Strictly, points of order are only relevant if there are standing orders covering the running of meetings; but that should not deter a skilful meeting manipulator. Argue that the discussion has strayed from the point of the agenda item, that extraneous issues are being raised, or that this discussion would be more appropriate under another item: anything to deflect continuing discussion.

◪ The concluding item on some agendas is "any other business", but the chairman may insist that only items previously notified can be discussed and that no papers can be tabled. No matter. Use the agenda item "date of the next meeting" to introduce a new topic, explain the issue, hand out the papers, express your opinion and suggest further discussion. Or propose a subcommittee or informal grouping to make recommendations.

◪ Formation of a subcommittee can also be proposed to prevent the meeting reaching an adverse decision: "We need to look into this issue with the care and attention it deserves." Make sure that the subcommittee has a majority of those who favour the idea.

◪ Calling for a postponement of discussion until the next meeting, on the grounds of lack of information, the need for more reflection, or until an absent member is present, can also be used to postpone a decision that seems likely to be decided against your interests. Calling for an adjournment of the meeting is a heavier version of the postponement device.

◪ If the ARTICLES OF ASSOCIATION or the rulebook of the CORPORATE ENTITY specifies a QUORUM, keep an eye on the number of people present. A lack of a quorum will totally stymie further debate.

◪ Hidden agendas – things that individuals want to achieve to benefit themselves or for their part of the organisation, rather than that of the whole organisation – can significantly affect the running of meetings.

The meeting manipulator's advice to a new director would be as follows.

- Forget rationality and what you learned in your MBA programme, influence not analysis is what counts in directors' meetings.

- Ignore the apparent issue on the agenda, set out to discover the cliques and cabals, find out who wields what power over whom.

- Make your presence felt, but carefully: "I wonder whether we might consider ..." not "these financials are a load of rubbish". "In my experience ..." is a better start to a contribution than "Surely everyone knows that ...".

- Propose alternatives rather than attack proposals on the table: "Another alternative might be ..." rather than "That'll never work in a month of Sundays."

(See also GAMES DIRECTORS PLAY.)

Memorandum of association

The formal, legal constitution governing a company. Typically, the memorandum will state the company's name, the location of its registered office, its objectives, that the liability of its members is limited and the amount and types of shares. Since a JOINT STOCK LIMITED LIABILITY COMPANY has a legal existence separate from its members, it is important for there to be a formal document that enables anyone contracting with the company to know its precise legal status. The memorandum, duly agreed by the founding members of the company, is filed with the companies' registration authority at the time of incorporation, and any subsequent change requires the approval of the SHAREHOLDERS.

www.companieshouse.gov.uk

Mentor

An experienced member of a board who accepts a responsibility, usually informally, to induct and guide a new member into the ways of the board and the company. The relationship can enable the new director to play his part more quickly and effectively.

Minutes

The formal record of a meeting, often kept by the COMPANY SECRETARY. Although there are no specific rules governing the content or format of minutes of board or board subcommittee meetings, they should provide a competent and complete record of what transpired and what was decided. Should there be a challenge, the minutes, duly approved as a true and fair report at a subsequent meeting, can be used as strong evidence of what was intended. Companies develop their own style in minute-keeping; for example, some boards note the names of the principal contributors to the discussion, others do not. In some cases, it has to be admitted, the minutes are no more than a staccato record of who attended and what was decided. At the other extreme, there are minutes that are almost a verbatim report of the proceedings, complete with stage directions. The ideal lies between the two. They should contain sufficient information to capture the main threads of the discussion, the options considered, the agreement reached and plans for action. The person responsible for writing the minutes potentially wields considerable power. (See MEETING MANIPULATION.)

Mission statement

A statement of the underlying purposes of a company, usually approved at board level. Typically, a mission statement will include references to the various STAKEHOLDERS in the business process – for example, suppliers, customers, SHAREHOLDERS, employees and, sometimes, broader societal interests. A well-developed mission statement can help the directors in the PERFORMANCE ROLES of STRATEGY FORMULATION and POLICYMAKING, because it establishes the desired relationship between the company and other parties that might be affected by board decisions. The danger of mission statements is that they can become little more than a public relations exercise, exhorting the company to do well by all of its stakeholders, despite inevitable conflicts of interest and without establishing the company's actual mission. (See also CORE VALUES.)

Monitoring management

Monitoring and supervising executive management is one of the principal components of a board's work. Indeed, many boards devote the major part of their time to this activity, perhaps to the detriment of the PERFORMANCE ROLES. A problem in monitoring management activity is striking the right balance between ensuring that management is pursuing the policies and plans agreed by the board and avoiding domination of executive decision-making. Monitoring management activities is often financially oriented, using data generated by internal management accounting and executive information systems. But financial measures can overemphasise short-term performance to the detriment of the board's responsibility for the longer-term development of the business. Increasingly, boards are seeing that they need non-financial measures of performance on matters such as customers' satisfaction, product development and employees' morale. It is also important not to rely solely on routine and standard performance reports. Briefings and presentations from non-board executives can be valuable sources of orientation and INFORMATION for directors, particularly outside directors. One of the challenges EXECUTIVE DIRECTORS face in monitoring management is that, effectively, they may be monitoring their own performance. Possible solutions are effective NON-EXECUTIVE DIRECTORS, a tough-minded CHAIRMAN and a professional BOARD STYLE. (See also EXECUTIVE SUPERVISION.)

Myners Report

A report on British pension fund investment. Paul Myners, its author, accused NON-EXECUTIVE DIRECTORS of failing to stand up to executives and suggested that they should meet formally with the five or six of the largest INSTITUTIONAL INVESTORS once a year, without company executives in attendance. The report called for a review of the role of the non-executive director, which led to the Higgs Report.

The old NatWest (Bank) board had 19 directors.
That is not a functional unit.
Paul Myners, former head of Gartmore Securities

NACD

See NATIONAL ASSOCIATION OF CORPORATE DIRECTORS.

NAPF

See NATIONAL ASSOCIATION OF PENSION FUNDS.

National Association of Corporate Directors

There is no common code of CORPORATE GOVERNANCE in the United States, although since the ENRON debacle various suggestions have been made. In 2002 the National Association of Corporate Directors (NACD) called for American stock exchanges to adopt a common code and identified ten core principles, including a split between the roles of CHAIRMAN and CEO (see DUALITY).

National Association of Pension Funds

An organisation representing the interests of British pension funds. The National Association of Pension Funds (NAPF) has taken a higher profile in CORPORATE GOVERNANCE issues in recent years, monitoring company activities against codes of good corporate governance conduct, occasionally advising on SHAREHOLDER ACTIVISM and PROXY VOTING options. A 2002 study showed that nearly half of the UK's top 400 companies failed to meet the recommendations of the COMBINED CODE. (See also ASSOCIATION OF BRITISH INSURERS.)

www.napf.co.uk

Communication is key. In the past companies have not understood shareholders. They in turn have wondered why a company hasn't explained its actions adequately in its annual report.
David Gould, NAPF

Nem. con.

Short for *nemine contradicente*, literally that no one is speaking against, or unanimous (see MEETING MANIPULATION).

New York Stock Exchange listing rules

The CORPORATE GOVERNANCE debacles of ENRON and WORLDCOM shook the complacent view that the United States had corporate governance systems that the rest of the world could well emulate. The SARBANES-OXLEY ACT introduced some significant legislative changes. The New York Stock Exchange (NYSE) proposed further changes to corporate governance standards through its *Listing Manual*.

Some essential elements of the new requirements are as follows.

- CEOs should certify each year that there are no violations of the NYSE listing standards.
- The board must have a majority of INDEPENDENT DIRECTORS.
- Boards must convene regular sessions for non-management directors to meet without executives present.
- A company must have an AUDIT COMMITTEE, a NOMINATING COMMITTEE and a REMUNERATION COMMITTEE consisting solely of independent directors.
- The CHAIRMAN of the audit committee must have an accounting or financial background.
- The audit committee must have sole responsibility for hiring and firing the company's outside independent auditors and for approving any non-audit work done by the audit firm.
- Independent directors must have no material relationship with the company; their companies must not do significant business with the company; and candidates may not join a board if they have worked for the company in the past five years.

- A five-year cooling-off period is required before a former employee of the company or its AUDITOR can be considered independent.
- Companies must adopt and disclose corporate governance guidelines on director qualifications, director responsibilities, director access to management, DIRECTOR REMUNERATION, director continuing education, management succession and an annual review of BOARD PERFORMANCE.
- SHAREHOLDERS must be given more opportunity to monitor and participate in the governance of companies.
- Shareholders' approval is needed for SHARE OPTION plans.
- Companies should establish orientation programmes for new board members and encourage continuing director education.

www.nyse.com

New directors should be equipped with an aggressive curiosity and a sensitive bullshit detector. They need a bit of scepticism that allows them to take unsentimental looks at the facts. They need their own data sources, access to information, to get a realistic picture. They often get insulated and think they owe the CEO. They forget it is the shareholders they are supposed to represent.
Jay Marshall, AlixPartners, 2002

Nominating committee

A subcommittee of the main board, made up wholly, or mainly, of independent OUTSIDE DIRECTORS, to make recommendations on new appointments to the board. It is an attempt to prevent the board becoming a cosy club, in which the incumbent members appoint like-minded people to join their ranks; a check-and-balance mechanism designed to reduce the possibility of a DOMINANT DIRECTOR, such as the CHAIRMAN or CEO, pushing through their own candidates. Nominating committees are widely used in major American companies. Unfortunately, the supposedly independent outside directors forming the committee are often themselves the choice of the chairman or CEO. Nevertheless, if board members are to work together as a tough-minded, effective team, it is just as well that they know each other. In the UK, although LISTED COMPANIES have adopted most of the requirements of the COMBINED CODE, the requirement to have a nominating committee has been resisted. This is not surprising, as the right to appoint to the board goes to the very heart of corporate power.

I am not happy with co-options to the board by the incumbent directors to fill casual vacancies that are put to the AGM merely for confirmation.
John Charkham, PRONED,
an organisation for Promotion of Non-Executive Directors

Nominee director

A director who is acting as a nominee for a major SHARE-HOLDER or other STAKEHOLDER, such as a venture capitalist or a bank investing in the company. The position of nominee directors can be fraught with difficulty, because all directors have a primary duty to act for the good of all the shareholders and not to take the part of any particular interested party. Furthermore, directors have a duty not to disclose privileged INFORMATION unless it is available to all the shareholders. It is important for a director who has been nominated and appointed to represent specific interests that his position is understood by the other directors. A director who receives confidential information, which is not available to the shareholders, must respect that confidentiality. Should a seriously contentious situation arise, a nominee director would be well advised to seek legal advice.

Non-executive director

A member of the board who is not employed by the company as an executive. The term is widely used in the UK and other countries in the Commonwealth, such as Australia, Hong Kong and Singapore. In the United States, the term OUTSIDE DIRECTOR is more frequently used. A basic tenet of good CORPORATE GOVERNANCE is that the non-executive directors (or NEDs) provide a check-and-balance mechanism on the executive directors. To achieve that, however, the non-executive directors also need to be independent of the company. In other words, they should have no relationship with the company, other than the directorship, that could be seen to influence the exercise of objective, independent judgment. This means that a director acting as a nominee for a major shareholder or a bank, someone linked to a firm in the company's ADDED-VALUE CHAIN such as a supplier or a distributor, a family member of the chief executive or a past employee of the company, cannot be seen to be independent. There may be a good case for such people to serve on the board as non-executive directors, but they cannot be seen to be independent. Particular challenges for non-executive directors are finding enough time to devote to the affairs of the company and knowing enough about the company's business and board-level issues.

www.nonexecutivedirector.com, www.uk.experian.com,
www.independentdirector.co.uk

N

Non-executive directors are the general manager's pet rocks.
Ross Perot

Non-executive directors are like bidets.
No one knows what they are for but they add some class.
Michael Grade, a non-executive director

What we want are non-executive directors who are geese not frogs. Frogs will sit motionless in water that is heated to boiling point, unaware of their situation, and taking no action until their ultimate demise.
Geese, as in Rome, honk loudly at impending crisis.
Christopher (Kit) McMahon, when deputy governor of the Bank of England

Relying on part-time outsiders is dangerous nonsense.
The idea has come about that in some manner non-executive directors can second-guess the executives. Of course they can't. The commercial

world would be in a far healthier state if all directors in listed companies worked within the business.

Lord Young, president, Institute of Directors, formerly a Conservative cabinet minister and chairman, Cable & Wireless

Non-profit entity

Non-profit enterprises or, as some prefer, not-for-profit organisations (recognising that for-profit enterprises do not always make a profit) may be incorporated formally as COMPANIES LIMITED BY GUARANTEE, in which case almost all of the material in this book will be relevant to their directors. Others may be created as trusts, when the requirements of trust law will apply, although many of the insights and ideas will also be useful. A particular challenge to boards of non-profit entities is determining what performance measures are appropriate, given that the bottom-line profit criterion, by definition, does not apply.

Non-voting shares

Shares which carry rights to contribute to and participate in the company's financial affairs but not the right to vote in company meetings. Such shares are not common and are usually offered to outside investors in companies in which SHAREHOLDERS who want to retain their dominant position hold control. Non-voting shares are not allowed under the LISTING RULES of most stock exchanges.

Occupational Pensions Board

An independent statutory body set up in the UK to ensure that pension schemes comply with statutory requirements and that pension schemes contracted out of the national procedures meet the minimum benefit requirements. It was caught out badly by MAXWELL.

OECD Principles

In May 1999, members of the Organisation for Economic Co-operation and Development (OECD) adopted the OECD Principles of Corporate Governance (see Appendix 2). These non-binding principles do not offer a universal CORPORATE GOVERNANCE system but are intended to serve as a reference point for countries' efforts to evaluate and improve their own legal, institutional and regulatory framework. In essence, the OECD principles call for the corporate governance framework to:

- protect the rights of SHAREHOLDERS;
- recognise the rights of STAKEHOLDERS and encourage active co-operation between companies and stakeholders in creating wealth, jobs and sustainability in companies;
- ensure timely and accurate DISCLOSURE on all material matters affecting the company, including the financial situation, performance, ownership and governance of the company;
- require the board to direct the company's strategy, monitor management effectively and be accountable to the shareholders.

www.oecd.org

Outside director

A term used in North America to describe a member of the board who is not an executive employee of the company. The term NON-EXECUTIVE DIRECTOR is used in the UK and most Commonwealth jurisdictions. An outside director should be a genuine outsider, that is, someone who is independent of the company, with no relationships (other than the directorship) that might be seen to affect the exercise of objective, independent judgment.

But what about the board? These guys were the illustrious guardians of the Ford Motor Company. They were supposed to constitute checks and balances to prevent flagrant abuse of power by top management. But it seems to me their attitude was: "As long as we're taken care of, we'll follow the leader." There's one mystery I want to unravel before I die: How can those board members sleep at night?

Lee Iacocca in his autobiography

The control of a large corporation is such a complex job and requires such constant attention that the outside board member, who has his own affairs to look after, can know very little about the business – too little on the whole to be useful as an outsider ... And an outside director in a large corporation cannot know enough to be specific, he must remain a figurehead.

Peter Drucker, *Concept of the Corporation*

Ownership

Ownership is the basis of power in the Anglo-American concept of the corporation. Formally, the SHAREHOLDER members of the company nominate and appoint the directors, who have a duty to exercise stewardship over the corporation for the benefit of the shareholders and to be accountable to them. Reality can be rather different. In large PUBLIC COMPANIES the membership is likely to be diverse, with both individual and institutional shareholders, whose objectives for dividend policy and capital growth differ and who are scattered geographically. The ability of owners to exercise power in such circumstances is severely limited. Various options have been suggested, such as TWO-TIER BOARDS with the SUPERVISORY BOARD reflecting, among other things, shareholder interests, or a CORPORATE

SENATE providing an intermediary shareholder committee. Some commentators want INSTITUTIONAL INVESTORS to exercise their power on behalf of all the owners. STAKEHOLDER THEORY calls for a rethink of the essentially 19th-century concept of the corporation to reflect the needs of 21st-century society. (See CORPORATE SENATE.)

In less than a century there is a serious question as to whether the modern corporate form has become obsolete ... How can one justify a system in which investors purchase shares in a company that is far too big and complex to permit any meaningful shareholder involvement in governance?
Robert Monks and Nell Minow, *Power and Accountability*

PAB

See PUBLIC COMPANY ACCOUNTING OVERSIGHT BOARD.

Pensions Investment Research Consultants

Pensions Investment Research Consultants (PIRC) represents over 60 INSTITUTIONAL INVESTORS with more than £350 billion under management. It has been a frequent source of SHAREHOLDER ACTIVISM in the UK, advising clients of issues (such as allegedly excessive DIRECTORS' REMUNERATION) and leading PROXY VOTING actions. PIRC also rates SHARE OPTION scheme and DIRECTORS' REMUNERATION reports, grading from A (acceptable) to C (advising that the directors' proposals be thrown out).

www.pirc.co.uk

Performance roles

Each UNITARY BOARD is responsible for the performance of the organisation, involving STRATEGY FORMULATION and POLICYMAKING, as well as fulfilling CONFORMANCE ROLES. The main performance roles can be thought of as follows.

Wise man The board respects the wisdom of the director, who brings accumulated knowledge and experience in business and elsewhere to bear on issues facing the board. Long-serving directors may well find themselves cast in this role by newer board colleagues. Accumulated wisdom can, of course, have limitations in fast-changing situations.

Specialist The director relies on his or her professional training, skills and knowledge to make a contribution. For example, the specialism could be in accountancy, banking, engineering, finance or law; or it could stem from specialist knowledge of a particular market, technology or functional area, such as marketing, manufacturing or personnel. In some newer, growing companies OUTSIDE DIRECTORS are appointed to the board specifically to provide such specialist inputs until such time as the company can afford to acquire these skills in-house at the executive level. When a board is relying on such expertise, it is important to ensure that the director remains in touch with the subject, which can sometimes prove difficult for those operating at board level.

Window-on-the-world The director is being used as a source of information on issues relevant to board discussions. Usually this will be on matters external to the company, such as insights into market opportunities, new technologies, industry developments, financial and economic concerns or international issues. Obviously, it is essential that the information is relevant, accurate and current. This is often a role specifically sought from outside directors, who are in a position to obtain such information through their other activities. A danger is that directors, chosen because of their access to specific information, lose touch with it.

Figurehead The director is called on to represent the company in the external arena; for example, in meetings with fund managers and financial analysts, or in trade and industry gatherings. The CHAIRMAN of the board often takes on this responsibility, perhaps being invited to join public committees, commissions and the governing bodies of important public institutions, as well as the boards of other non-competing companies. A figurehead for the company is also increasingly important for many companies in dealing with the media.

Contact person This is an important role often played by outside directors, who are able through their personal contacts to connect the board and senior management to networks of potentially useful people and organisations. For example, the director might be needed to forge contacts in the world of politics and government; link the company with relevant banking, finance or stock exchange connections; or make introductions within industry or international trade. This role typically supplements the window-on-the-world role, but adds a more proactive dimension. Politicians are sometimes offered directorships on the assumption that they have useful contacts and influence in the corridors of power.

Status provider In the past, eminent public figures were often invited to join boards just to add status, rather than for any specific contribution they could make to board deliberations. A knight-hood in the UK or service as a senator in the United States almost guaranteed invitations to join PUBLIC-COMPANY boards. In today's business climate, business acumen, professionalism and the ability to contribute directly to board affairs are vital. More-over, exposure to LITIGATION deters some public figures from ac-cepting merely honorary directorships. But even today, if a company has been experiencing high-profile problems, it can help restore confidence if a status provider with a reputation for integrity is appointed to the board.

Peters Report

A committee set up under the auspices of the Dutch Association of Securities-Issuing Companies and the Amsterdam Stock Ex-change Association, which reported in 1997 on corporate governance in the Netherlands, a country that uses SUPERVI-SORY BOARDS. The report made some 40 recommendations on the composition, task, appointment, remuneration and method of working of both the supervisory and executive boards. Better ACCOUNTABILITY, increased transparency and a more profes-sional way of working were recommended for the Dutch system of CORPORATE GOVERNANCE.

PIRC

See PENSIONS INVESTMENT RESEARCH CONSULTANTS.

Point of order

Some organisations establish formal rules for the orderly conduct of meetings. Typically, such rules provide for partici-pants in the meeting to appeal to the CHAIRMAN on a "point of order" should they feel the rules are not being followed. (See also MEETING MANIPULATION.)

Poison pill

A device for foiling a hostile takeover. For example, the terms of a company's ARTICLES OF ASSOCIATION may include provisions that:

- reduce the voting power of any shares once a holder acquires, say, 30%;
- provide a high-return security to existing SHAREHOLDERS should a bid not be recommended by the board;
- introduce convertible stock on which the conversion terms change on an unwelcome bid.

To ensure a free MARKET FOR CONTROL, some jurisdictions try to outlaw poison pills.

Policymaking

Policies enable strategies to be implemented. For example, a company may need a set of market policies that lay down the ground rules on matters such as pricing, service and customer relations. Without such policies, management might take decisions that are contrary to the STRATEGIC INTENT. It might be necessary to have product policies to cover, for example, product safety, innovation and quality; financial policies to cover credit and debt collection, borrowing limits and gearing, spending controls and management approval limits, inventory control and working capital management; and employment policies to lay down the criteria for worker safety, pay and conditions, and the company's attitude towards trade unions. Some companies have written policies for social responsibility, which detail the firm's commitment, for example, towards minority rights, pollution control or the environment generally.

Policymaking is one of the principal elements of the board's PERFORMANCE ROLES. In business circles, it is usual to talk of policies stemming from strategies; for example, a company, having decided to pursue a strategy of product differentiation, will need appropriate pricing policies, customer relations policies and product safety policies. In government circles, the terms can be reversed; for example, a government talks of pursuing a policy of tax reduction through various strategies such as cutting tax rates or through higher allowances.

Portfolio analysis

A professional CORPORATE PLANNING technique which enables directors to locate their product portfolio in a matrix comparing market share (and thus the ability to generate cash flow) with market potential (the likelihood of growth). A jargon has grown up around portfolio methods. Firms were enabled, for example, to identify and distinguish their products as "stars", "cash cows", "dogs" and those with "potential". Star products had high market share and continuing potential; cash-cow products also had large market shares but their life cycle was in decline, so they could be milked to provide the funds to invest in those products which had potential, but low market share as yet. Dogs had neither current market standing nor future potential and should be removed from the portfolio. Such methods were based on a belief that all products had life cycles, which should be reflected in corporate strategies. Experience has shown that although portfolio analysis can give directors some useful insights, it does not produce strategies. The theory of product life cycles was found to be too simplistic and, organisationally, it proved difficult to find managers who were prepared to see the profits that they had created "milked" to feed other parts of the company.

President

A title often held in conjunction with that of CHAIRMAN. The precise responsibilities and powers vary considerably. It is used more widely in American companies than elsewhere.

Président directeur-général

The powerful sole head of many French companies in which the UNITARY BOARD is normal but not mandatory.

Private company

Many company law jurisdictions differentiate between a PUBLIC COMPANY and a private company. Private companies, typically, are not allowed to make public invitations to subscribe for shares and have to limit the number of shareholders (50 in the UK). In recognition of their special status, the regulatory requirements for private companies, for example on the filing and DISCLOSURE of information, are less demanding. Some jurisdictions recognise a further subcategory of private company for small companies or CLOSELY HELD COMPANIES (in which the owners, directors and managers are closely related), giving further concessions such as relaxing AUDIT requirements if all the SHAREHOLDERS agree.

Privatisation

There are two different meanings.

1 The decision by the directors of a LISTED COMPANY to make it private again by buying back the shares that are in the hands of the public. Fortnum and Mason, a superior food shop in London, after 62 years on the stockmarket, returned to private hands in 2001.
2 The privatising of enterprises that had previously been run as nationalised industries. Often this process starts with the creation of a CORPORATE ENTITY, with a board of directors to run the business on market-oriented, profit-driven criteria, followed by privatisation with the shares floated on the stockmarket. The UK and New Zealand pioneered the process, which has been followed in many other countries. Telecommunications, power utilities, water supply, airlines, railways

and shipping companies have all been privatised. In the UK, some people are suggesting that privatisation has gone too far, citing problems with Railtrack, which effectively went bankrupt, and other utilities, caused by the investment needed to meet public expectations and the difficulties of providing universal service, such as supplying remote areas at below true market cost. These challenges are usually tackled by establishing a REGULATOR and through government subsidy.

Proxy voting

Under typical ARTICLES OF ASSOCIATION, SHAREHOLDERS have the right to appoint proxies to vote on their behalf on the resolutions before general meetings of shareholders. In earlier times, this typically meant voting on the reappointment of directors and AUDITORS, accepting the annual accounts and agreeing the dividend to be paid. In recent years, particularly in the United States and increasingly in the UK, dissatisfied shareholders have used the proxy mechanism to promote their concerns, calling for the removal of CHAIRMEN and CEOS, attacking the level of DIRECTORS' REMUNERATION and introducing other critical resolutions.

P

Public company

A company that is permitted to invite the public to subscribe for its shares. By definition, all companies listed on a stock exchange are public companies; but a public company need not be listed and may attract its SHAREHOLDERS, such as venture capitalists, by other means. Recognising the benefits a public company enjoys, most jurisdictions require more extensive filing, DISCLOSURE and information access than is required of a PRIVATE COMPANY. In the 19th century, in the early days of the corporate concept, all companies were public companies. Today, although public companies are usually the more significant firms, and some of them are huge, they account for less than 5% of all companies.

Public Company Accounting Oversight Board

The regulating body for the American accounting profession, created in 2002 by the SECURITIES AND EXCHANGE COMMISSION following the ENRON and WORLDCOM debacles. The Public Company Accounting Oversight Board (PAB) was to be independent of the accounting firms, thus effectively ending the American accounting profession's long-established system of self-regulation, although the accounting industry tried to staff the oversight board with allies. William Webster, the PAB's newly appointed CHAIRMAN, resigned at his first meeting following criticism of his connection with a company accused of fraud; this also contributed to the resignation of Harvey Pitt, the chairman of the SECURITIES AND EXCHANGE COMMISSION.

www.sec.gov

Quasi-government enterprise

The move towards cost-effectiveness in government in many countries has led to developments such as CORPORATISATION, PRIVATISATION and outsourcing. One result has been the creation of various quasi-governmental institutions to facilitate, monitor and regulate these activities. Many of the CORPORATE GOVERNANCE issues discussed in this book apply to the members of such boards, committees and councils, even though they may not have the formal title of director.

Quorum

The minimum number of members who need to be present, under the ARTICLES OF ASSOCIATION or other rules of a CORPORATE ENTITY, to make a meeting quorate, thus legitimising it (see MEETING MANIPULATION.)

Regulator

A state-wide company registrar function, needed in all company law jurisdictions, to ensure that companies are properly incorporated, listed on the company register and continue to meet the various requirements to avoid being struck off, such as filing periodic returns and financial reports. The company registrar provides one of the basic controls in CORPORATE GOVERNANCE. For a PUBLIC COMPANY listed on a stock exchange, the listing committee of the exchange also exercises a regulatory function ensuring compliance with that exchange's LISTING RULES. State regulators may also be necessary where state utilities and other state business enterprises have been privatised.

Federal law in the United States has much less to say on the duties of company boards than on day-care centres.
Nell Minow, www.corporateboard.com

Regulatory capture

A too close relationship between a regulatory body and the profession, industry or company it is regulating, which can erode the independence and objectivity of the REGULATOR.

Related party transaction

A business transaction between a company and a party closely related to it, such as a director or a major SHAREHOLDER; for example, the purchase by the company of a property from one of its directors. The LISTING RULES of most stock exchanges require related party transactions to be disclosed and, often, approved by the other shareholders.

Relationship investor

An INSTITUTIONAL INVESTOR who takes a significant, long-term stake in a LISTED COMPANY with a view to being closely involved and intending to have a close relationship with the board. A good example is Warren Buffett, whose Berkshire Hathaway Fund invests in a handful of companies for the long term, intending to exercise some influence over the company. Sometimes the relationship investor will have a NOMINEE DIRECTOR on the board. Some might argue that relationship investing represents a return to the original concept of SHAREHOLDER DEMOCRACY and power; but others note that a relationship investor is able to influence the board while the other shareholders lack that INSIDE INFORMATION and influence.

> *Relationship investing contrasts sharply with the stereotype of the American shareholder who is depicted as an off-track bettor with no interest in the horse beyond the results for the daily race.*
> *"Betting slip" shareholding is not a promising base for responsible ownership. The combined status of ownership and commercial relationship gives particular investors a sufficiently significant stake to ensure an effective presence.*
> Robert Monks

> *I've always said my favourite time frame for holding a stock is forever. I don't buy stocks with the idea of selling them unless I'm in arbitrage ... I only invest in companies within my circle of competence: I don't mind missing opportunities from firms I don't understand.*
> Warren Buffett, Berkshire Hathaway Fund

> *A good director is one who has a meaningful financial stake in the venture ... (as) there is nothing that makes a director think like a shareholder more than being a shareholder.*
> Warren Buffett, Berkshire Hathaway Fund

Remuneration committee

A committee of the main board, consisting wholly or mainly of independent OUTSIDE DIRECTORS, with the responsibility for overseeing the remuneration packages of board members and, possibly, members of senior management. DIRECTORS' REMUNERATION remains a concern around the world. The problem is how to provide sufficient incentive to directors, rewarding success, while avoiding the label FAT CAT. Even a remuneration committee composed entirely of outside directors may not be thought independent if its members are nominated by the CHAIRMAN or CEO and are themselves senior executives of other companies.

> *Shareholders should have access to details of directors' remuneration.*
> *This would end the charade of "you come on my board and*
> *I'll come on yours" – or rather "you come on my remuneration*
> *committee and I'll go on yours".*
> Lord Young, president, Institute of Directors,
> formerly a Conservative cabinet minister and chairman, Cable & Wireless

Remuneration ratcheting

Directors can use various arguments to justify high board-level rewards. These include the following.

International comparator "To ensure that our company attracts and holds executive directors of the calibre we need against international competition, we have to give rewards that are broadly comparable to those they could obtain in the industry anywhere in the world." This argument is advanced even if the directors concerned have never been headhunted in their lives and whether or not they have any possibility of working abroad.

Headhunter "We have just recruited a new finance director and the headhunters assured us that he had to receive a package that is 30% more than that of the highest-paid director. Of course, we all had to have an increase to maintain differentials." This argument conveniently overlooks the fact that the fee of the headhunter is based on 30–35% of the first year's salary of the new appointee.

Top of the industry "Our firm prides itself on being one of the leaders in the industry, even though at the moment we are not among the most profitable. We expect to pay our directors in the upper quartile of the industry range as shown by the comparator pay research." This argument totally ignores the performance of the firm or the directors.

Fear of loss "We could lose our directors to the competition unless we pay competitive rates." This argument is sometimes advanced even though the directors concerned are within a year or two of retirement and would be of absolutely no interest to competitors.

Doubling up the bonus "We believe that it is important for directors' rewards to be performance-related. Moreover, we expect excellent performance in both the short and the long term. So we calculate bonuses on the annual profits, then we have a parallel three-year scheme which rewards directors if earnings per share grow by 30% over that period." This way the directors get rewarded twice on the same performance, inflation is ignored and there is no upside cap should there be exceptional circumstances. Moreover, directors do not get penalised for poor performance.

In the UK, the United States and some other countries there are now specialist consultants offering advice to companies on appropriate levels of reward. Some also advise the fund managers of INSTITUTIONAL INVESTORS who, increasingly, monitor DIRECTORS' REMUNERATION and take action when it seems out of line. (See also REMUNERATION COMMITTEE.)

Representative board

A board whose members are the direct nominees of specific SHAREHOLDERS or are appointed to represent the interests of various groups of shareholders. In the case of a CORPORATE ENTITY without shareholders, it is a board whose members represent the interests of members; for example, the committee of a Canadian agricultural co-operative with members representing growers, buyers and sources of finance. Representative boards are frequently found in NON-PROFIT ENTITIES, where the directors are elected to serve the interests of various interest groups; for example, in a UK hospital trust, to represent patients, doctors, nursing staff, the health authority and the local community.

Representative director

See NOMINEEE DIRECTOR and JAPANESE CORPORATE GOVERNANCE.

Responsibilities of directors

See FIDUCIARY DUTY and DUTY OF CARE.

Risk management

Although the phrase might seem an oxymoron, risk management has become an essential part of a board's work. A risk management policy identifies and prepares a response to unexpected risks, such as product hazards, corporate fraud, environmental pollution, employees' injuries, business interruption (through fire or internet interference, for example), LITIGATION risk and reputation risk, including being tainted by a customer's lack of honesty. The TURNBULL REPORT, now incorporated in the UK's COMBINED CODE on CORPORATE GOVERNANCE, emphasised the board's responsibility for managing risk.

R

Rival camps

See GAMES DIRECTORS PLAY.

Roles for directors

Although all directors have the same responsibility to act for the good of the company, in practice different members of the board play different roles according to their knowledge, experience and expertise. A balanced board will have members appointed for the different qualities they can bring to the job, such as technical skills, knowledge or good contacts. (See CONFORMANCE ROLES and PERFORMANCE ROLES.)

Rubber-stamp board

A form of BOARD STYLE in which directors act solely to confirm decisions taken by executive management or the holding company in a group.

Sarbanes-Oxley Act

The sound of stable doors closing. This law was rushed through in 2002 in the United States after a series of CORPORATE GOVERNANCE scandals including ENRON and WORLDCOM. The new rules are regulated by the SEC and apply to all companies, including overseas companies, quoted in the United States. CEOs and chief financial officers are required to certify under oath that their financial statements neither contain an "untrue statement" nor omit any "material fact". AUDIT COMMITTEES must have totally INDEPENDENT DIRECTORS. AUDITORS are not allowed to undertake lucrative non-AUDIT work, including keeping accounting records, information systems work, actuarial services, internal audit outsourcing services, management functions including human resources, and other legal and expert services unrelated to the audit. The Sarbanes-Oxley Act (SOX) has been criticised as an overreaction and condemned as extraterritorial legislation by overseas companies listed in the United States. Lawyers may be its main beneficiaries.

Safety valve

One of the roles a director can play (see CONFORMANCE ROLES).

SEC

See SECURITIES AND EXCHANGE COMMISSION.

Secret profit

A director must not make a secret profit out of dealings with the company, for example through private interests in a contract in which the company is involved. Directors have a duty to disclose any such interests to the board and to abide by their decision on what is in the company's best interest.

Securities and Exchange Commission

An American body set up in 1934 to protect SHAREHOLDERS from overambitious company promoters and unscrupulously powerful incumbent boards. Over the years the DISCLOSURE, regulatory and investigative processes of the Securities and Exchange Commission (SEC) have increased, and the United States now has the most expensive (and the most litigious) corporate regulatory regime in the world. The belief of many Americans that their corporate regulatory system was the envy of the world and should be widely adopted elsewhere took a serious knock following the ENRON and WORLDCOM debacles. Harvey Pitt, the CHAIRMAN on watch when these problems became apparent, resigned after 15 months in the job, following a public row over the appointment of the head of the new PUBLIC COMPANY ACCOUNTING OVERSIGHT BOARD and allegations of close relations with the accountancy profession.

> Q: How should America's securities law be reformed?
> A: By a simple two-part law.
> Section one: it shall be unlawful.
> Section two: the SEC shall have the power to define "it".
> Harvey Pitt, when chairman of the SEC

Senate

See CORPORATE SENATE.

Shadow director

Occasionally, a person exercises power over a company's affairs although he is not actually on the board. Although not formally a director, the other board members operate in his shadow. Often this is the founder and significant SHAREHOLDER, who remains in the shadows to escape the DISCLOSURE requirements of directorship. However, in some jurisdictions shadow directors can be held responsible for their actions as though they actually are directors.

> *Options are a one-way bet. If a company's share price goes up, the holder of the options can make a serious fortune.*
> *If the share price falls, the holder of the option doesn't lose a penny.*
> *Nothing risked, everything to gain.*
> Sunday Times, November 2002

Share option

Share options are often awarded to directors as part of their remuneration. These options give them the right to buy shares in their company at a predetermined price, sometime in the future, after the share price has risen. The intention is to provide an incentive to increase SHAREHOLDER value, which has been reflected in the higher share price. In the United States, it is standard practice to issue share options to both executive and OUTSIDE DIRECTORS. In the UK, options are typically given to EXECUTIVE DIRECTORS, although Hermes, one of the UK's largest fund managers, has suggested that NON-EXECUTIVE DIRECTORS should receive half their remuneration in shares. Share options can provide a strong incentive to directors to increase their company's share price. Unfortunately, this includes a strong incentive to bolster the share price artificially. Options provided a significant incentive to directors of companies in the high-tech and dotcom boom, hastening such companies' demise. They also played a part in the downfall of ENRON and WORLDCOM. Some problems with options are as follows.

- **Dilution** of the value of other shareholders' shares occurs as additional shares are issued to meet the options. This may be insignificant if the exercised options represent only a small part of the total share capital; but if they represent a large part, as can occur in smaller companies, the effect may be significant.
- **Reloading** can occur if a company repeatedly gives its directors further options whenever they exercise the ones

they hold. This may encourage them to play the market, rather than concentrating on the longer-term improvement of corporate performance.

- **Resetting** involves lowering the price at which the option can be exercised as share prices fall. Obviously, an option becomes less attractive as the current price falls towards the option's price. If bid prices are lowered in this way, the incentive reward is lost.
- **Rewarding mediocrity**. A good incentive should reward better-than-average performance on the part of the recipient of the option. But share prices reflect general rises in the stockmarket as well as the specific performance of the company. Indeed, the share price can rise even though the company is doing badly.

Accounting for share options remains a contentious topic. In some countries boards treat them as though they are free. In fact, as extra shares are issued other holdings are diluted. Options taken up by directors (and other employees) have a value, hence they have a cost, which should be reflected in the company's accounts. There is no respectable argument against this principle, although vested interests in the United States blocked the 1994 proposals of the FINANCIAL ACCOUNTING STANDARDS BOARD to reflect this cost. The INTERNATIONAL ACCOUNTING STANDARDS BOARD has proposed that from January 2004 share options should be charged in company accounts, thus becoming a charge against profits. Although the valuation of options remains contentious, some UK companies are accounting for them: one of the first was HSBC.

Enron was a huge success for its top managers. Kenneth Lay, chairman and CEO, made $123m in 2000 from exercising share options.
The Economist, January 5th 2002

Shareholder

The owner of shares in a company. The ARTICLES OF ASSOCI-ATION of a company may authorise various classes of share, including ordinary shares, preference shares (which give holders preferential rights to dividends and/or on winding-up) and other more specialised types of shares. The shareholder VOTING RIGHTS attached to each class of share determines the potential governance power in the company. Company law lays down the information that must be provided to all shareholders. Traditionally, this was delivered in printed prospectuses, regular directors' report and financial accounts and other required notices; but increasingly communication can be through electronic means. (See also DUAL VOTING RIGHTS.)

Shareholder activism

See SHAREHOLDER POWER.

Shareholder democracy

Ownership of shares is the basis of power in a JOINT STOCK LIMITED LIABILITY COMPANY. Normally, the ARTICLES OF ASSOCIATION provide SHAREHOLDERS, voting on resolutions before shareholder meetings, with one vote for each share they hold. Although many refer to this as shareholder democracy, in reality it is shareholder plutocracy, power exercised according to wealth, since in a democracy, the people (*demos*) have one vote each. There have been calls for power over companies to be exercised in this way (see CORPORATE SENATE). Other ideas for improving SHAREHOLDER POWER through shareholder watchdog boards have included a shareholder panel, proposed by the Auditing Practices Board in the UK, a CORPORATE GOVERNANCE board, proposed in the Australian Senate, and a conflicts board, proposed in the United States in the University of Michigan's *Journal of Law Reform*.

www.aph.gov.au/senate, www.corpmon.com, www.shareholderaction.org, www.corpwatch.org

Shareholder power

In a private CLOSELY HELD COMPANY, the SHAREHOLDERS and the directors are often close, even the same people, so the shareholders can readily influence board decisions. However, individual shareholders in PUBLIC COMPANIES seldom have real power in governance matters. In the major LISTED COMPANIES, shareholdings are widely dispersed and geographically spread. Even with shareholder interest groups and better opportunities to communicate with the other members, individual investors usually lack the position, prestige or power to influence an incumbent CHAIRMAN and his board. RELATIONSHIP INVESTORS seek to overcome this problem. But an INSTITUTIONAL INVESTOR, even with a small holding, can influence boards, particularly if it acts in concert with others. However, the interests of different types of institutional investors do not necessarily coincide; for example, some may be looking for a quick profit and others may want to take a longer-term view. There is also a potential problem: if institutional investors get too close to the board, share-price-sensitive INSIDE INFORMATION may be obtained (see, for example, CALPERS and PIRC).

www.corpmon.com, www.shareholderaction.org, www.corpwatch.org,
www.hermes.co.uk

Hermes' corporate governance programme is founded on a belief that companies with interested and involved shareholders are more likely to achieve superior long-term performance than without. Tied closely with this is the belief that a company run in the interests of shareholders will need to manage effectively links with its employees, suppliers and customers, to behave ethically and have regard for the environment and society as a whole.
www.hermes.co.uk

Electronic reporting will become the norm for companies, enfranchising the ultimate owners of capital, leading to cheaper costs of capital and ultimately driving a democratisation of shareholder relations.
Paul Myners, former head of Gartmore Securities

Shareholder value

The boards of many LISTED COMPANIES are committed to maximising the value of their shareholders' equity, a commitment reinforced by the HAMPEL REPORT. But the measurement and management of shareholder value is not a straightforward accounting calculation. Several methodologies are used, including value-based management (VBM), economic value added (EVA) and shareholder value added (SVA). But, essentially, all measurements of shareholder value recognise that historical, profit-based measures fail to take into account the cost of the capital that has been used and offer variations on measures of the present value of future cash flows, discounted at the average cost of capital. Trends in share prices and dividend payouts are often taken as a short-term surrogate for shareholder value. Unfortunately, efforts to enhance shareholder value can lead to board-level short-termism that limits vital research and development, strips out assets and employees to meet the company's long-term goals and outsources vital functions.

Shell company

A LISTED COMPANY whose shares are not currently traded on the stock exchange. On some exchanges, if control is obtained over such a company, the listing can be used to obtain a quotation for another business enterprise, without incurring the cost and exposure of a full prospectus, by "backing" the other business into the shell. This is sometimes called a BACKDOOR LISTING.

Snowing

See GAMES DIRECTORS PLAY.

Sokaiya

A member of a YAKUSA gangster organisation in Japan, used to disrupt companies' annual general meetings. *Sokaiya* were originally employed to ensure that no one asked awkward questions (the average length of shareholder meetings in Japan is still just over 15 minutes). But sometimes disputes arise over their remuneration and trouble ensues. A famous meeting of the Sony Corporation lasted 13 hours with chairs as well as abuse being thrown. Some companies pay off the *sokaiya* to avoid the disruption of their meetings, but the Japanese government clamped down on these payments to improve the image of the financial sector.

SOX

The acronym adopted in the United States for the SARBANES-OXLEY ACT, named after the two congressmen who sponsored it.

Special purpose entity

A legal entity created by a company to structure its finances. Legitimate reasons for setting up a special purpose entity (SPE) include the offsetting of risk, obtaining tax benefits and raising capital from partners. However, financial engineering through SPES have caused problems for the setters of accounting standards, including the lack of DISCLOSURE, obscurity and the distortion of financial statements by taking indebtedness off the parent company's balance sheet. ENRON had set up nearly 1,000 SPES, many in the Cayman Islands tax haven.

One Enron SPE was Raptor, a partnership between Enron and some Enron executives. Enron lent Raptor $500m in Enron stock. Raptor then issued an IOU to Enron, which Enron guaranteed, promising to pay more stock if Raptor could not repay. Enron then treated this promissory note as an asset on its balance sheet. In other words, Enron had used its own equity shares on one side of its balance sheet to create an asset on the other. Raptor then borrowed funds secured on its Enron stock-holding and invested in Avici, a computer-network manufacturer. As Raptor's investments increased in value, Enron recorded a $500m profit, although no profit had actually been realised. Then the investment in Avici lost value. Raptor could not repay the IOU and called on the guarantee. Enron then had to pay in its own stock, which was also falling, so more and more stock was needed to pay the debt. Although Raptor did not appear as an asset or a liability on Enron's balance sheet, Enron had recorded a $500m profit from it and, subsequently, had to recognise a massive loss of capital in it. This contributed to Enron's demise.

Special purpose vehicle

The term frequently used in the UK for a SPECIAL PURPOSE ENTITY. (See also ENRON.)

Specialist

One of the roles a director can play (see PERFORMANCE ROLES).

Spinning

Bankers launching an INITIAL PUBLIC OFFERING of shares might "spin" an allotment to friends at beneficial prices, then, once the price has risen, "flip" the shares to less fortunate buyers. Citigroup told congressional investigators that it had allocated IPO shares to Bernie Ebbers, former boss of WORLD-COM, which was a big client, insisting that this was not a bribe but a reward for a good client. Goldman Sachs was also accused of providing business clients with cheap shares in "hot" companies on the London stockmarket at the expense of other investors. US securities REGULATORS investigated spinning following the market collapse of 2000–02. (See GAMES DIRECTORS PLAY for an alternative meaning.)

Sponsorship

See GAMES DIRECTORS PLAY.

Staggered board

A board whose members' terms of appointment are staggered, so that only a proportion (often one-third) retire each year; sometimes called a classified board. Staggered appointments bring greater stability to a board, allowing directors more freedom to take a longer-term view of strategic issues. Critics of staggered boards complain that hostile bidders cannot remove an entire board at a single election. Staggered boards therefore become a takeover defence, entrenching underperforming directors. Annual election allows a change of control through a single successful proxy contest. Consequently, resolutions opposing staggered boards and calling for declassification have topped shareholder activists' calls for change.

A key question currently confronting the Congress is whether something is so fundamentally wrong with the structure of corporate governance that it requires legislative remedy. In principle, corporations are run for the benefit of shareholders, within the context of laws that are designed to protect the rights of third parties. Such protections, whether for employees, the community or the environment, should not be obligations of corporate management. They are appropriately left to statute.
Alan Greenspan, Wall Street Journal, 2002

Stakeholders

Groups whose interests are affected by a company's activities. The primary stakeholder group recognised by law in most jurisdictions is the SHAREHOLDERS. Other stakeholders include company employees, whose rights are protected by employment law; creditors and those with non-equity financial stakes in the company, who are protected by contract law; and groups in a company's ADDED-VALUE CHAIN, such as suppliers, subcontractors, agents, distributors and the ultimate customers. Some people add local, national and international societal interest groups to the list of stakeholders.

The old cry of "what about the workers?" is being replaced by a new call "what about the stakeholders?" But it is important to distinguish directors' accountability from their responsibility.
Andrew Pettigrew, Warwick Business School, November 1997

Stakeholder theory

A body of ideas pursued initially in the 1970s and early 1980s. In the *Corporate Report*, a study commissioned by British accounting bodies in 1975, it was suggested that major corporations had a duty to be accountable to all those who might be affected by their actions, including employees, suppliers, customers and communities, as well as SHAREHOLDERS. The political dimensions of the proposals resulted in considerable criticism and the shelving of the proposals. Ira Millstein and Salem Katsch, writing in 1981, offered a more objective insight into the issues:

This strident and partisan concept of substantially unrestrained corporate power and discretion is, in a more moderate form, among the most important fundamental public concerns within large corporations ... at issue is whether the nation ... will accept larger private corporate size, accelerate the decline of pluralism by regulating or by giving greater responsibility to government, or by requiring fundamental changes in the internal governance structure of our major corporations.

Stakeholder thinking faded in the free-market growth ethos of the 1980s but subsequently reappeared (see TOMORROW'S COMPANY).

No business exists in a vacuum. We are conscious of the influence our business has on communities, throughout the UK both locally and nationally. If a community as a whole flourishes, the individual members of that community tend to flourish too.
Sir Colin Southgate, quoted in the RSA Inquiry report, *Tomorrow's Company*

Status provider

One of the roles a director can play (see PERFORMANCE ROLES).

Stewardship theory

The original theory underpinning company law recognises that directors can be trusted to exercise a FIDUCIARY DUTY towards the company, acting as stewards of the SHAREHOLDERS' interests, which they place ahead of personal ambition. Thus stewardship theory runs contrary to the ideas of AGENCY THEORY, which proposes that individual directors, given the chance, will maximise their own utility and cannot be expected to adopt a stewardship perspective if checks and balances are not put in place.

Saying that we work for our shareholders may sound simplistic – but we frequently see companies that have forgotten the reason they exist. They may even try to be all things to all people and serve many masters in many different ways. In any event they miss their primary calling, which is to stick to the business of creating value for their owners.

Roberto Goizueta, former head of Coca-Cola

Stock option

See SHARE OPTION.

Strategic alliance

Strategic alliances with other companies are the preferred way for many companies to enter markets, transfer technology, procure supplies or manufacture products around the world, or share risk on an international scale. Sometimes the partners in the strategic alliance are competitors in other fields. Many alliances involve the incorporation of a joint-venture company owned by two or more partner companies. Directors of such joint-venture companies are typically drawn from the senior management of the partners. Governing joint-venture companies can present special challenges. Disagreements not envisaged in the initial joint-venture agreement can arise between the partners. Directors then face conflicts of interest between their responsibilities to the joint-venture company and to the partner company that employs them. Moreover, many joint-venture companies are incorporated in foreign jurisdictions, with diverse and different company laws and regulatory regimes, and have overseas partners with different cultures.

Strategic intent

The underlying drive of a board of directors to achieve strategic success in the longer term. It might be, for example, to become the largest company in the software industry, to be the best airline in the world or to put a specific competitor out of business. Strategic intent enables a company to make the most of its CORE COMPETENCIES, to establish CORE VALUES throughout the organisation that unite everyone to the common goal, and to achieve better results than would have occurred had the board merely sought to fit their resources to the strategic situation.

Strategic vision

Directors need a shared perception of the future for their company, a perspective that encapsulates their aspirations for the enterprise. Some call this a strategic vision. It reflects what the board wants to achieve; the direction they want the organisation to take; where they want the enterprise to be in the future. "When you don't know where you're going, all roads lead you there." Information about the strategic context is, obviously, fundamental to this process. One of the important developments in the provision of INFORMATION at board level in recent years has been the creation of customer and competitor information systems. These monitor not what is going in inside the company, as most traditional management information systems do, but what is going on outside in the strategic milieu. Sometimes a strategic vision is articulated in no more than a general statement of overall aims (see STRATEGIC INTENT); in other cases, quantified aims or goals are determined. Of course, a strategic vision remains no more than a dream unless management can turn it into reality.

The strategies of many entrepreneurial firms are hidden. The strategic success of business leaders such as Richard Branson (Virgin), Bill Gates (Microsoft) and Rupert Murdoch (News Corporation) often stems from emergent, unexpected and innovative strategies. They recognise strategic opportunities and are capable of reacting quickly. Such business leaders often create their boards of directors to give them support or to meet stockmarket expectations. The directors' contributions to strategy may be confined to providing information and giving advice, as long as the company continues its strategic success. But, of course, not all strategic visionaries remain successful. Henry Ford nearly destroyed the car business he had built up brilliantly by a failure to delegate and change as the business grew.

The board of a large public corporation is an inappropriate body for developing strategy, setting corporate culture and policy and initiating major decisions. Instead the board should concentrate on the critical review of proposals, with management having the primary duty to formulate and then implement proposals.

Hilmer Report, *Strictly Boardroom*, 1993

S

Strategy formulation

Setting the direction for the business, in the context of the external competitive and customer market situation, and in the light of prevailing economic, political and technological factors. This is a crucial aspect of the board's role; it is after all why directors are so called.

Strategy formulation is typically an iterative process leading from perceptions of the strategic situation, through possible strategies, choices, projects, plans, implementation and outcomes. Strategic thinking is continual, and strategies emerge over time, rather than being created by a deliberate planning process.

The crucial discovery in formulating corporate strategy, which had been known by military strategists for thousands of years, was that it is not possible to create strategies for an organisation until the strategies being pursued (and capable of being pursued) by rival (and potential rival) organisations are understood. Company-centred planning systems often fail to adopt this perspective. HELICOPTER VISION is needed to see the business in the context of its competitors and customers, and of the political, economic, social and technological setting.

Other strategies need to be developed, evaluated and, eventually, the directors have to make choices. Then the chosen strategies must be supported by appropriate POLICYMAKING, which lays down the guidelines for management. In formulating strategy and making related policy, a particular challenge to directors is to ensure that the long-term interests of the company are balanced with the short-term goals. Pressure to show strong performance in annual (even quarterly) directors' reports can all too easily adversely affect the pursuit of strategies that would fit the company for a better strategic future.

A significant trend in recent years has been away from strategies that emphasise business as a battlefield with global competitors, towards searching out strategic allies with whom mutually beneficial STRATEGIC ALLIANCES can be built.

In earlier days, when change and strategic challenge came fairly slowly, CORPORATE PLANNING was often an annual process, associated with the budget preparation. Today, strategy formulation, in most professionally led companies, is a continuous activity for senior management and the directors. Strategies often emerge as strategically significant information is digested and strategic options are discussed. Some boards of directors delegate much of the strategy formulation to the CEO and senior management. The outside directors act more as catalysts, probing the management's proposals, questioning their assumptions, challenging their conclusions, until a consensus is reached. Other boards are more closely involved in the details of strategic thinking. Recognising the importance of board-led strategic thinking, directors seem increasingly to be devoting specific board time and effort to strategy formulation, both during BOARD MEETINGS and by creating specific strategy sessions, often away from the boardroom.

> *All men can see the tactics whereby I conquer: but none can see the strategy out of which victory is evolved.*
>
> Sun Tze, *The Art of War*, 6th century BC

Suboptimisation

See GAMES DIRECTORS PLAY.

SUNBEAM CORPORATION

In 1996 Sunbeam, an American appliances manufacturer, was in serious financial trouble. Al Dunlap, known as "Chainsaw" Al for his approach to cutting staff, was appointed to save the company. Over the next two years the business reported dramatically improved results. Investors chased after the shares as the price rocketed. There was talk of a bid, which would make the investors, particularly Dunlap and his colleagues, a lot of money. But no bid came.

By 1998 some OUTSIDE DIRECTORS were uneasy and launched an inquiry. Dunlap was fired. The SECURITIES AND EXCHANGE COMMISSION subsequently charged him, other senior executives and the AUDIT partner at ANDERSEN, who had approved the accounts, with fraud. The SEC alleged that, on his arrival, Dunlap identified massive previous losses which he wrote off, giving him a "cookie jar" to dip into to inflate subsequent results. Then he shipped out more goods through his distribution channels than could possibly be sold, taking credit for the revenue but pushing forward the problem to the next financial year. Returned goods were overlooked. Other efforts were made to boost sales artificially; for example, a record number of outdoor barbecues were sold during the winter months.

In 2001 Andersen agreed to pay $110m to Sunbeam's shareholders in settlement of a lawsuit alleging that the AUDITORS had failed to identify the problem. The directors had a FIDU-CIARY DUTY to protect the interests of SHAREHOLDERS, but they failed. Resignation is seldom a sufficient response.

Supervisor

One of the roles a director can play (see CONFORMANCE ROLES).

Supervisory board

The upper board in the TWO-TIER BOARD approach to CORPORATE GOVERNANCE. In the continental European model, the supervisory board monitors and supervises the performance of the executive board. Its power is derived from the ability to hire and fire the CEO and other members of the executive. Common membership of the supervisory board and the executive board is not allowed. Some protagonists argue that the supervisory board distinguishes between the PERFORMANCE ROLES and CONFORMANCE ROLES that can become confused in a unitary board. (See also GERMAN CORPORATE GOVERNANCE.)

S

Sustainable development

The new orthodoxy of strategic thinking around the world. Sustainable development meets the needs of the present without compromising the ability of future generations to meet their own needs. Stemming from radical environmental movements of the 1970s, which offered apocalyptic visions of the earth's future, sustainable development today is being embraced by boards as part of their strategic thinking. Some companies report regularly to their shareholders on the sustainable implications of their longer-term plans (for an example see www.mtr.com.hk). The GLOBAL REPORTING INITIATIVE, established by the American environmental lobby CERES and backed by the UN, aims to provide companies of all sizes and in all markets with a template for reporting on sustainability issues, including the environment, labour practices, corruption, human rights, and health and safety. (See also CORE VALUES, CORPORATE SOCIAL RESPONSIBILITY and ETHICS.)

www.globalreporting.org, www.wbcsd.ch

Corporate sustainability is a business approach that creates long-term shareholder value by embracing opportunities and managing risks deriving from economic, environmental and social development.
Dow Jones Sustainability Indexes, www.sustainability-index.com

---

SWOT analysis

A tool of CORPORATE PLANNING, which involves taking a rigorous review of the Strengths and Weaknesses that a company has and the Opportunities and Threats that it faces. The technique is still used by many boards, although its fundamental weakness is that it is company-centred. In rapidly changing strategic situations, the strategist must consider the strategies of competitors and customers and in the context of its industry (see HELICOPTER VISION and STRATEGY FORMULATION).

Titles

Not all people who carry the title of director are directors; and some who are not called director may be held liable as though they are. Titles such as director of long-range planning may add status and director of private banking may add authority, but they do not necessarily imply membership of the board. Such people would be ASSOCIATE DIRECTORS. Conversely, a SHADOW DIRECTOR, although not formally having the title of director, can influence board decisions and may be held responsible, in law, for the exercise of that power.

Tokenism

The inclusion of directors on the boards of PUBLIC COMPANIES because they reflect (and can be seen to reflect) minority or other STAKEHOLDER interests, such as ethnic background, consumers or the environment, rather than because of any specific contribution they might make to the board's work. Tokenism was at its height during the stakeholder debates of the 1970s, particularly among American corporations. Some NOMINATION COMMITTEES still recommend members with such backgrounds, but primarily because of their potential to contribute to the board's work, not because of their background.

TOMKINS

Greg Hutchings had built Tomkins, a heavily diversified British group, from scratch, through a series of daring takeovers. It included Rank Hovis McDougall, a baking business, and Smith and Wesson, a handgun manufacturer.

Hutchings was chief executive from 1984 to 2000 and the dominant decision-maker. Although the board had a separate CHAIRMAN, Hutchings was alleged to have treated the company as his private domain, enjoying a lavish lifestyle at the company's expense, with corporate jets, corporate properties and corporate entertaining. His wife and his housekeeper were on the payroll. His own bonus was tied to the dividend, and was thus determined by decisions of the board that he dominated.

But the share price had been underperforming the market, as had the company. Investors were uneasy. INSTITUTIONAL INVESTORS called for a refocus in the strategy and for a strengthened independent board. There were threats to replace the senior management team. The finance director resigned. A new chairman and a tough OUTSIDE DIRECTOR were appointed. At the AGM in September 2000, questions were asked about the benefits provided by the company to Hutchings. Within weeks he "resigned". He claimed that he had had the approval of the previous chairman and the board for all his decisions and an inquiry by Ernst & Young (not the company's AUDITORS) found that Hutchings's pay and perks had indeed been within his contract.

The lessons of this case are that such concentration of power falls short of the standards now expected of directors of public LISTED COMPANIES. DOMINANT DIRECTORS of companies funded by public SHAREHOLDERS, particularly successful founder directors, need a critical, tough-minded and independent board, capable of setting appropriate standards of corporate behaviour, raising vital questions and taking appropriate action when dissatisfied with the answers.

Tomorrow's Company

T The title of a report published in the UK in 1995 by the Royal Society of Arts. Written by a group of business people, the report argued that successful companies did not act solely for the benefit of SHAREHOLDERS but took an inclusive view of the interests of other STAKEHOLDERS (without using that word), including customers, suppliers and employees. The HAMPEL REPORT took a different view, arguing that although a company had to satisfy its customers, suppliers and employees, it is accountable to its shareholders.

Shareholder value is the imperative commanding a lot of attention, but you cannot create shareholder value by talking to your shareholders. You create it by looking at the four drivers of a successful business: how good you are at involving and motivating your staff; how close you are to your customers; how good you are at removing wastage from the supply chain and maintaining good relations with suppliers; what your reputation is in the community at large. We don't believe that the board is there purely to create shareholder value. I'm sure nobody leaps out of bed in the morning and says "I want to create shareholder value!" It's unrealistic.

Sir Stuart Hampson, chairman,
John Lewis Partnership and Tomorrow's Company

Tracking stocks

Some companies in traditional industries created tracking stocks to reflect the profits of attractive subsidiary companies in more highly valued new industries. General Motors created the first tracking stock in 1984 to track the profits in its computer subsidiary. Tracking stocks, sometimes called designer stocks, enable a company to realise the value in an attractive subsidiary without actually spinning it off and floating it separately. The parent company continues to own the assets and to control the subsidiary company. Since tracking stocks were typically valued higher than the parent stock, firms could raise capital. Furthermore, companies could offer incentive options to employees of a subsidiary in the stock tracking their own profits. However, tracking shares can involve complex accounting and management problems, and Wall Street has a hard time valuing them. Unfortunately, some stocks were tracking businesses in high-tech industries which have subsequently collapsed.

Triple bottom line

See CORPORATE SOCIAL RESPONSIBILITY.

Turnbull Report

A report on CORPORATE GOVERNANCE in the UK, which explored some issues raised by the HAMPEL REPORT in more depth, particularly the board's responsibility for RISK MANAGEMENT. The COMBINED CODE incorporated the findings of the Turnbull Report.

www.dti.gov.uk/cii, www.icaew.co.uk/internalcontrol, www.iia.org.uk,
www.globalcommunity.org

Two-hat dilemma

The potential problem facing all EXECUTIVE DIRECTORS: in the boardroom are they wearing the hat of a director responsible for the governance of the company as a whole, or are they wearing their executive hat representing the interests and defending the performance of their part of the organisation?

I make it clear to all my executive directors that when they are in my boardroom they take off their executive hat and accept responsibility with me for the direction of the company as a whole
Lord Caldecote, when chairman of the Delta Group

Two-tier board

A governance structure, found in some continental European countries, including Germany and the Netherlands, in which the executive board comprising the senior executive team is entirely separate from the upper SUPERVISORY BOARD. (See also GERMAN CORPORATE GOVERNANCE.)

The same reason which induced the Romans to have two consuls makes it desirable for there to be two chambers of parliament; that neither of them may be exposed to the corrupting influence of undivided power.
John Stuart Mill

TYCO

Dennis Kozlowski became chief executive of Tyco, based in New York, in 1992. Treating the company as a private fiefdom, he siphoned off some hundreds of millions of dollars in private expenditure, including the running costs of his antique racing yacht, insurance for nine houses, two powerboats and eight cars, and a gold and burgundy shower curtain. Kozlowski's compliant board gave him a contract saying that he would not be dismissed if convicted of a felony, unless it directly damaged the company. Subsequently, it transpired that he had also authorised funding $4m to support a chair in CORPORATE GOVERNANCE at Cambridge University in the UK. He claimed that this was jointly funded by the company and himself. Some irate Tyco shareholders, hoping to retrieve some of their squandered funds, tried to recover these university funds. But the university authorities insisted that studies in corporate governance were necessary and that they could put the funds to good use.

UK Combined Code

See COMBINED CODE.

Unitary board

Company law in some jurisdictions requires a company to have a single board of directors. This could consist entirely of EXECUTIVE DIRECTORS (as in some family companies), entirely of OUTSIDE DIRECTORS (as in some companies established for charitable purposes) or a mix of executive and NON-EXECUTIVE DIRECTORS. In the United States, big companies usually have a majority of independent, outside directors. In the UK, executive directors used to form a majority on the board, but the trend is towards BOARD STRUCTURES with a majority of non-executive directors. By contrast, a company incorporated in some continental European jurisdictions has a TWO-TIER BOARD.

Vice-chairman

A title used by some boards to spread the work of the CHAIR-MAN; by others to mark the chairman-elect; and by a few to confer prestige without necessarily giving additional responsibilities or powers.

Chairman, Vice-chairman, President – the titles do not always mean quite what they seem. Analysing the hierarchies at the top of American public companies can be a little like working out where real power lies in the Kremlin. The man at the top of the pecking order may, indeed, be the big potato, but it is just as likely that he counts for nothing at all.
Robert Lacey, *Detroit's Destiny*

Viénot Report

A report on CORPORATE GOVERNANCE in France, published in 1995. It recommended that:

Every board should set up an accounts or audit committee to ensure that the accounting methods used in preparing the accounts are pertinent and consistent, and should inform the AGM of its existence and the number of times it had met during the year.

VODAFONE/MANNESMANN

The first hostile takeover by a foreign firm in German corporate history occurred in 2000 when Vodafone, a British company, made a successful bid for Mannesmann, a German company. Mannesmann used the classic GERMAN CORPORATE GOVERN-ANCE structure, with a wholly executive board overseen and appointed by a SUPERVISORY BOARD, which had both SHARE-HOLDERS and employee representatives.

An acrimonious meeting of the Mannesmann shareholders followed the acquisition. They claimed that severance bonuses of around £50m, paid as part of the bid negotiations to Klaus Esser, head of Mannesmann, and other senior executives, were immoral, reduced the company's value and had been designed to influence the bid. "Crooks" and "looters" were two of the epithets hurled at members of both the executive and supervisory boards.

Klaus Zwickel, a member of the supervisory board and head of IG Metall, the metalworkers' union, protested that the bonuses were "indecently high", until it was pointed out that he was present and voted in favour of them at the supervisory board meeting. Initially, Vodafone said it knew nothing of the bonuses, but later conceded that the idea had come from Hong Kong-based Hutchinson Whampoa, one of Mannesmann's major shareholders, and that Vodafone had agreed to permit such payments provided that they were made legally.

In Anglo-American corporate governance, an open MARKET FOR CONTROL, which assists takeover activity, is seen as essential to a healthy capital market. The potential of a hostile bid for underperforming companies can act as an important motivator to boards. For over a decade, the European Union had been trying to develop Europe-wide laws that would facilitate hostile bids and restrict company defences against them. But in Germany hostile takeovers are viewed with suspicion by both management and unions. The Mannesmann case reinforced this opinion. Under pressure from companies and trade unions, the German government actively sabotaged the EU proposals, offering instead its own weaker set of controls, which, effectively, permit some defensive actions if backed by the company's supervisory board. Germany has sound governance structures but substandard DISCLOSURE practices. There is a need for a process that is more transparent and allows an open market in corporate control.

In 2003, after a two-year investigation, charges alleging breach of trust were brought against members of the Mannesmann supervisory board, including the heads of both Deutsche Bank and IG Metall.

Voluntary organisations' governance

See NON-PROFIT DIRECTORS.

Vorstand

The executive committee or board in the German TWO-TIER BOARD system (see GERMAN CORPORATE GOVERNANCE).

Voting rights

The ARTICLES OF ASSOCIATION of a company usually provide the terms and procedures for members' voting in its general meetings. If a meeting votes by a show of hands, those present have a vote each and the size of individual shareholdings will not count; if a poll is called for, the typical clause in the articles provides for one vote for each share. (See also PROXY VOTES and DUAL VOTING RIGHTS.)

Voting with their feet

The tendency of some INSTITUTIONAL INVESTORS to prefer not to become involved in the governance issues of companies in which they have invested, reserving the right to sell the shares rather than voting their shares and becoming involved in governance issues. (See also RELATIONSHIP INVESTING.)

War room

Some boards have their boardroom fitted out with display screens and information-retrieval facilities to provide information pertinent to decisions under discussion. However, the analogy with the military operations room in a battle situation is suspect, since military operations involve real-time tactical responses as situations evolve, whereas the time horizon of board-level decisions is usually long-term and strategic.

WASTE MANAGEMENT

In 1992 ANDERSEN, the AUDITOR of Waste Management, an American refuse-collection company, identified some improper accounting practices which had resulted in an overstatement of reported profits. These misstatements totalled $93.5m, which was less than 10% of reported profit. Furthermore, one-off gains of over $100m, which should have been shown separately in the accounts, had been netted against other expenses. A "clean" AUDIT certificate was signed.

In 1993 Andersen identified further misstatements of $128m, which represented 12% of reported profit. Again it decided that these misstatements were not sufficiently material for the audit report to be qualified. But it did decide to allow the company to write off prior misstatements over a number of years, instead of making immediate DISCLOSURE as required by GENERALLY ACCEPTED ACCOUNTING PRINCIPLES. In 1994 the company continued its practice of netting expenses against one-off gains.

Waste Management was an important and lucrative client for Andersen. Between 1991 and 1997 audit fees totalled $7.5m, and other fees, such as consulting services, contributed $11.8m. In Andersen's words, Waste Management was a "crown jewel" among its clients. Moreover, Waste Management's senior finance executives had all previously been Andersen auditors.

In June 2001, the SECURITIES AND EXCHANGE COMMISSION brought actions against Andersen and four of its partners in connection with its audits of the annual financial statements of Waste Management for the years 1992–96. These statements, on which Andersen issued unqualified or "clean" opinions, overstated Waste Management's pre-tax income by more than $1 billion.

The SEC found that Andersen "knowingly or recklessly issued false and misleading audit reports ... [which] falsely stated that the financial statements were presented fairly, in all material respects, in conformity with generally accepted accounting principles". Without admitting or denying the allegations or findings, Andersen agreed to pay a civil penalty of $7m, the largest ever SEC enforcement action against a then big-five accounting firm.

This case raises the vexed issue of auditors' independence. Andersen had a close relationship with a valuable client, which led to creeping year-on-year acceptance of less than acceptable auditing standards. The SEC's director of enforcement commented: "Andersen and its partners failed to stand up to company management and thereby betrayed their ultimate allegiance to Waste Management's shareholders and the investing public."

Watchdog

One of the roles a director can play (see CONFORMANCE ROLES).

White knight

In a hostile takeover bid, the attacked company may look for another, more acceptable company – a white knight – to protect it with a counter-offer.

W

Window dressing

See GAMES DIRECTORS PLAY.

Woman director

More women than before are becoming directors of major British organisations, although the numbers are still small and most of them are NON-EXECUTIVE DIRECTORS.

> *Women directors used to be in politics or good works: today they are younger, with relevant business experience.*
>
> Viki Holton, *Corporate Governance*, Vol. 3, No. 2, 1995

Worker director

Proponents of industrial democracy argue that governing a major company involves an informal partnership between labour and capital, and that consequently labour should be represented in the CORPORATE GOVERNANCE processes. In a German SUPERVISORY BOARD, for example, half of the members are chosen under the CO-DETERMINATION laws through the employees' trade union processes. In the 1970s, the draft Fifth Directive of the European Community (now the European Union) proposed supervisory boards with employee representation for all large companies. The BULLOCK REPORT was the British response. Since then the company law harmonisation process in the EU has been overtaken by social legislation, including recent requirements that all major firms should have a WORKS COUNCIL through which employees can participate in significant strategic developments and policy changes. Most EU member countries have already adopted this legislation; others must follow.

Works council

W

The European Union's company law harmonisation process, in its draft Fifth Directive, originally proposed WORKER DIRECTORS on the boards of companies incorporated in the EU. However, the Social Chapter of the Maastricht treaty has overtaken the idea of worker directors. Large companies in the EU must have a works council and inform and consult with employees on strategic issues and plans that might affect employment. From 2005, any firm in the EU with 150 or more staff will have to inform and consult its workers about business and employment prospects. The limit will reduce to 50 or more employees in 2008.

> *I think compulsory works' councils are a waste of time and money because most large companies have consulting mechanisms, so it's an attempt to reinvent the wheel.*
> Richard Wilson, Institute of Directors, 2000

WORLDCOM

"WorldCom systematically flouted the rules of accounting and lied outright to investors", according to the Justice Department, when investigating the collapse of this huge American company. The company was founded by Bernie Ebbers, a charismatic entrepreneur, whose first job as a boy was delivering milk in Canada. He followed this with a basketball scholarship at Mississippi College, and work as a basketball coach, nightclub bouncer and motel owner. In 1983 he saw the opportunity to create a long-distance telecommunications carrier by buying capacity from the newly deregulated AT&T. It is said that he scrawled his vision on a restaurant table napkin.

The build-up

Long Distance Discount Services (LDDS) was formed and Ebbers spent the next 18 years building a global telecoms powerhouse, mainly through acquisitions. These included TCL Telecom, a major player in Ireland, SkyTel's paging business and UUNET Technologies, an internet backbone operation that carries half of America's internet traffic. Then in 1997 Ebbers gazumped BT to acquire the long-distance phone business of MCI, a company three times its size, for $37 billion. By 2000, WorldCom had more than 20m customers in over 200 countries.

The acquisitions were nearly always paid for in WorldCom shares, which Ebbers believed would continue to surge in value in the new information age. An exception was the purchase of BT's share in MCI, which BT insisted was bought for cash, a wise decision that made BT over £2 billion, instead of a massive loss had they taken and held on to WorldCom shares.

Ebbers's personal wealth grew with the massive growth of WorldCom's share price, at its peak reaching over $60 a share. Moreover, he gambled on it increasing further, taking from the company a personal loan of $343m to meet a call on WorldCom shares he had bought.

In April 2002 he resigned. The compliant board agreed a generous severance package: a $22m GOLDEN HANDSHAKE, $1.5m a year for life, the continuation of his low-interest loan now standing at $408m and unlimited use of the company's jet. Later, as the debacle unfolded, the board reviewed these terms. John Sidgmore, who had previously run UUNET Technologies, became chief executive following Ebbers's resignation. He was a hard-driven man, who claimed he needed only three hours' sleep a night.

Unwelcome revelations

The revelation that over the past five quarters $3.8 billion of expenditure, which should have been charged against annual profits, had been capitalised came in June 2002. The accounts, which should have disclosed a significant loss, showed a profit of $1.4 billion. The extent of the fraud was increased to $9 billion after a SECURITIES AND EXCHANGE COMMISSION investigation revealed inflation of profits since 1999.

ANDERSEN, WorldCom's AUDITOR, had been dismissed, following the adverse publicity of the firm's handling of the ENRON audit. When WorldCom's internal auditors discovered the accounting irregularities, Cynthia Cooper, vice-president of internal audit, alerted KPMG, the new external auditor.

Three members of the accounting staff were indicted for fraud by a federal grand jury: Scott Sullivan, the chief financial officer; Burford Yates, the former director of general accounting; and David Myers, the former controller who was dismissed in June 2002. Sullivan stepped down and exercised his constitutional right not to testify to a Congressional inquiry. Ebbers also invoked the Fifth Amendment, but told Congress he had done nothing wrong, and the investigations did not link him directly with the fraud.

Bankruptcy protection under Chapter 11 was sought in July 2002. This was the largest filing in corporate history, surpassing even Enron. The share price collapsed; 17,000 jobs were lost worldwide.

Most of WorldCom's $422 billion debt was in corporate bonds, mainly held by INSTITUTIONAL INVESTORS around the world. They were appalled. Many pension funds, concerned at the fall in the equity market, had switched to the supposedly less erratic bond market. CALPERS admitted a $330m unrealised loss on WorldCom bonds. Yet many IN-VESTMENT ANALYSTS had been promoting WorldCom shares to the very end.

Bert Roberts Jr, WorldCom's CHAIRMAN, who had deflected calls from investors and creditors for his resignation, stood down in November 2002, opening the way for a wholesale clear-out of the boardroom.

What went wrong?
Unlike Enron, WorldCom's failure was basically a result of a classical accounting fraud: its accounts did not conform to GEN-ERALLY ACCEPTED ACCOUNTING PRINCPLES. In governance terms, this was a company that seemed to meet many of the guidelines on good CORPORATE GOVERNANCE. The chairman-ship and the CEO's roles were split between different people, unlike in most American companies. A majority of the board members were OUTSIDE DIRECTORS.

But look more closely: of the 12 directors, five were World-Com executives but two more worked for companies acquired by WorldCom; Max Bobbitt, chairman of the AUDIT COMMIT-TEE, had benefited from selling WorldCom shares and, at the time of the collapse, held nearly 500,000 shares. This was a board with a dominant founder-director lacking truly independent and tough-minded outside members. Directors were beholden to and sycophantic towards Ebbers, who some now suggested was an overbearing buccaneer, who took pride in his lack of technical knowledge of the telecoms industry.

A corporate culture of fiddling the figures also emerged. Sales staff had increased the reported revenues by registering a single sale many times over, paying the salesman commission on each occasion, in a practice known as "rolling the revenues".

The only experience Bernie Ebbers had operating a long-distance carrier is that he used the phone.

A friend commenting on the founder of WorldCom

I continued to be positive about WorldCom because it fits my thesis of what a strong, valuable company should be.

Jack Grubman, an investment analyst accused of bias in favour of WorldCom

Yakusa

Japanese underworld organisations often run in a business-like, corporate manner. The *yakusa* sometimes threaten disruption of companies' ANNUAL GENERAL MEETINGS if they are not suitably rewarded. Consequently, many companies hold their AGMs on the same day.

Zaibatsu

Closely related networks of Japanese companies, which oper-
ated in the early years of the 20th century. After the second
world war the occupying forces sought to disband the *zaibatsu*
because of their previous close connections with military
central powers. Of the 325 *zaibatsu* companies originally ear-
marked to be broken up, however, only 11 were dismantled.
Some of the present-day *keiretsu* reflect these earlier relationships, particularly Japanese banks, which were not reformed.
(See JAPANESE CORPORATE GOVERNANCE.)

Appendices

1 The UK Combined Code of Best Practice and Principles of Governance

The various codes of good practice in corporate governance in the UK (the Cadbury, Greenbury, Hampel and Turnbull Reports) were combined and included as part of the London Stock Exchange listing requirements in 1998. Listed companies are required to make a two-part corporate governance report to their shareholders. In the first part, a company explains how the principles have been applied, in the light of any special circumstances that apply. The form of the report is not prescribed; companies have a free hand to explain their approach to corporate governance. In the second part, a company confirms that it has complied with the code of best practice or explains why it has not.

The following material provides the principles and major extracts from the code. (To avoid unnecessary detail, just the principles are given for sections B, C and D.)

A Directors

1 The board
Principle
Every listed company should be headed by an effective board, which should lead and control the company.

Code provisions
A1 The board should meet regularly.
A2 The board should have a formal schedule of matters specifically reserved to it for decision.
A3 There should be an agreed procedure for directors in the furtherance of their duties to take independent professional advice if necessary, at the company's expense.
A4 All directors should have access to the advice and services of the company secretary, who is responsible to the board for

ensuring that board procedures are followed and that applicable rules and regulations are complied with. Any question of
the removal of the company secretary should be a matter for
the board as whole.

A5 All directors should bring an independent judgment to bear
on issues of strategy, performance, resources, including key appointments, and standards of conduct.

A6 An individual should receive appropriate training on the
first occasion that he or she is appointed to the board of a listed
company, and subsequently as necessary.

2 Chairman and CEO

There are two key tasks at the top of every public company: the
running of the board and the executive responsibility for the
running of the company's business. There should be a clearly
accepted division of responsibilities at the head of the
company, which will ensure a balance of power and authority,
such that no one individual has unfettered powers of decision.

Code provisions

A7 A decision to combine the posts of chairman and chief executive officer in one person should be publicly explained.
Whether the posts are held by different people or by the same
person, there should be a strong and independent non-executive element on the board, with a recognised senior member
other than the chairman. The chairman, chief executive and
senior independent director should be identified in the annual
report.

3 Board balance

The board should include a balance of executive and non-executive directors (including independent non-executives) such
that no individual or small group of individuals can dominate
the board's decision-taking.

Code provisions

A8 The board should include non-executive directors of sufficient calibre and number for their views to carry significant
weight in the board's decisions. Non-executive directors should

comprise not less than one-third of the board.

A9 The majority of non-executive directors should be independent of management and free from any business or other relationship which could materially interfere with the exercise of their independent judgment. Non-executive directors considered by the board to be independent should be identified in the annual report.

4 Supply of information

The board should be supplied in a timely manner with information in a form and of a quality to enable it to discharge its duties.

Code provisions

A10 Management has an obligation to provide the board with appropriate and timely information, but information volunteered by management is unlikely to be enough in all circumstances and directors should make further enquiries where necessary. The chairman should ensure that all directors are properly briefed on issues arising at board meetings.

5 Appointments to the board

There should be a formal and transparent procedure for the appointment of new directors to the board.

Code provisions

A11 Unless the board is small, a nomination committee should be established to make recommendations to the board on all new board appointments. A majority of the members of this committee should be non-executive directors and the chairman should be either the chairman of the board or a non-executive director. The chairman and members of the nomination committee should be identified in the annual report.

6 Re-election

All directors should be required to submit themselves for re-election at regular intervals and at least every three years.

Code provisions
A12 Non-executive directors should be appointed for specified terms and reappointment should not be automatic. All directors should be subject to election by shareholders at the first opportunity after their appointment, and to re-election thereafter at intervals of no more than three years. The names of directors submitted for election or re-election should be accompanied by biographical details.

B Directors' remuneration

1 The level and make-up of remuneration
Levels of remuneration should be sufficient to attract and retain the directors needed to run the company successfully. The component parts of executive directors' remuneration should be structured so as to link rewards with corporate and individual performance.

2 Procedure
Companies should establish a formal and transparent procedure for policy on executive remuneration and for fixing the remuneration packages of individual directors. No director should be involved in fixing his or her own remuneration.

3 Disclosure
The company's annual report should contain a statement of remuneration policy and details of each director's remuneration.

C Relations with shareholders

1 Dialogue with institutional shareholders
Companies should be ready, where practicable, to enter into a dialogue with institutional shareholders based on the mutual understanding of objectives.

2 Constructive use of AGMs
Companies should use the AGM to communicate with private investors and encourage their participation.

D Accountability and audit

1 Financial reporting
The board should present a balanced and understandable assessment of the company's position and prospects.

2 Internal control
The board should maintain a sound system of internal control to safeguard shareholders' investments and the company's assets.

3 Relationship with the auditors
The board should establish formal and transparent arrangements for considering how they should apply the financial reporting and internal control principles and for maintaining an appropriate relationship with the company's auditors.

2 The OECD Principles of Corporate Governance

The principles represent a common basis that the Organisation for Economic Co-operation and Development (OECD) member countries consider is essential for the development of good governance practice. The OECD intends the principles to provide guidance and suggestions for stock exchanges, investors, corporations and other parties that have a role in the process of developing good corporate governance, as well as assisting member and non-member governments in their efforts to evaluate and improve the legal, institutional and regulatory framework for corporate governance in their countries. The principles focus on publicly traded companies. However, they might also be a useful tool to improve corporate governance in non-traded companies, for example, privately held and state-owned enterprises.

1 The rights of shareholders

The corporate governance framework should protect shareholders' rights.

A Basic shareholder rights include the right to:
1 secure methods of ownership registration;
2 convey or transfer shares;
3 obtain relevant information on the corporation on a timely and regular basis;
4 participate and vote in general shareholder meetings;
5 elect members of the board; and
6 share in the profits of the corporation.

B Shareholders have the right to participate in, and to be sufficiently informed on, decisions concerning fundamental corporate changes such as:
1 amendments to the statutes, articles of incorporation or similar governing documents of the company;

2 the authorisation of additional shares; and

3 extraordinary transactions that in effect result in the sale of the company.

C Shareholders should have the opportunity to participate effectively and vote in general shareholder meetings and should be informed of the rules, including voting procedures, that govern general shareholder meetings.

1 Shareholders should be furnished with sufficient and timely information concerning the date, location and agenda of general meetings, as well as full and timely information regarding the issues to be decided at the meeting.

2 The opportunity should be provided for shareholders to ask questions of the board and to place items on the agenda at general meetings, subject to reasonable limitations.

3 Shareholders should be able to vote in person or *in absentia*, and equal effect should be given to votes whether cast in person or *in absentia*.

D Capital structures and arrangements that enable certain shareholders to obtain a degree of control disproportionate to their equity ownership should be disclosed.

E Markets for corporate control should be allowed to function in an efficient and transparent manner.

1 The rules and procedures governing the acquisition of corporate control in the capital markets, and extraordinary transactions such as mergers and sales of substantial portions of the corporate assets, should be clearly articulated and disclosed so that investors understand their rights and recourse. Transactions should occur at transparent prices and under fair conditions that protect the rights of all shareholders according to their class.

2 Anti-takeover devices should not be used to shield management from accountability.

F Shareholders, including institutional investors, should consider the costs and benefits of exercising their voting rights.

2 The equitable treatment of shareholders

The corporate governance framework should ensure the equitable treatment of all shareholders, including minority and foreign shareholders. All shareholders should have the opportunity to obtain effective redress for violations of their rights.

A All shareholders of the same class should be treated equally.
  1 Within any class, all shareholders should have the same voting rights. All investors should be able to obtain information about the voting rights attached to all classes of shares before they purchase. Any changes in voting rights should be subject to shareholder vote.
  2 Votes should be cast by custodians or nominees in a manner agreed upon with the beneficial owner of the shares.
  3 Processes and procedures for general shareholder meetings should allow for equitable treatment of all shareholders. Company procedures should not make it unduly difficult or expensive to cast votes.

B Insider trading and abusive self-dealing should be prohibited.

C Members of the board and managers should be required to disclose any material interest in transactions or matters affecting the corporation.

3 The role of stakeholders in corporate governance

The corporate governance framework should recognise the rights of stakeholders as established by law and encourage active co-operation between corporations and stakeholders in creating wealth, jobs and the sustainability of financially sound enterprises.

A The corporate governance framework should assure that the rights of stakeholders that are protected by law are respected.

B Where stakeholder interests are protected by law, stakeholders should have the opportunity to obtain effective redress for violations of their rights.

C The framework of corporate governance should permit performance-enhancing mechanisms for stakeholder participation.

D Where stakeholders participate in the corporate governance process, they should have access to relevant information.

4 Disclosure and transparency

The corporate governance framework should ensure that timely and accurate disclosure is made on all material matters regarding the corporation, including the financial situation, performance, ownership and governance of the company.

A Disclosure should include, but not be limited to, material information on:
  1 the financial and operating results of the company;
  2 company objectives;
  3 major share ownership and voting rights;
  4 members of the board and key executives, and their remuneration;
  5 material foreseeable risk factors;
  6 material issues regarding employees and other stakeholders;
  7 governance structures and policies.

B Information should be prepared, audited and disclosed in accordance with high-quality standards of accounting, financial and non-financial disclosure, and audit.

C An annual audit should be conducted by an independent auditor in order to provide an external and objective assurance on the way in which financial statements have been prepared and presented.

D Channels for disseminating information should provide for

fair, timely and cost-effective access to relevant information by users.

5 The responsibilities of the board

The corporate governance framework should ensure the strategic guidance of the company, the effective monitoring of management by the board, and the board's accountability to the company and the shareholders.

A   Board members should act on a fully informed basis, in good faith, with due diligence and care, and in the best interest of the company and the shareholders.

B   Where board decisions may affect different shareholder groups differently, the board should treat all shareholders fairly.

C   The board should ensure compliance with applicable law and take into account the interests of stakeholders.

D   The board should fulfil certain key functions, including:

1   Reviewing and guiding corporate strategy, major plans of action, risk policy, annual budgets and business plans; setting performance objectives; monitoring implementation and corporate performance; and overseeing major capital expenditures acquisitions and divestitures.

2   Selecting, compensating, monitoring and, when necessary, replacing key executives and overseeing succession planning.

3   Reviewing key executive and board remuneration, and ensuring a formal and transparent board nomination process.

4   Monitoring and managing potential conflicts of interest of management, board members and shareholders, including misuse of corporate assets and abuse in related party transactions.

5   Ensuring the integrity of the corporation's accounting and

financial reporting systems, including the independent audit, and that appropriate systems of control are in place, particularly systems for monitoring risk, financial control and compliance with the law.

6 Monitoring the effectiveness of the governance practices under which it operates and making changes as needed.

7 Overseeing the process of disclosure and communications.

E The board should be able to exercise objective judgment on corporate affairs independent, in particular, from management.

1 Boards should consider assigning a sufficient number of non-executive board members capable of exercising independent judgment to tasks where there is a potential for conflict of interest. Examples of such key responsibilities are financial reporting, nomination, and executive and board remuneration.

2 Board members should devote sufficient time to their responsibilities.

F In order to fulfil their responsibilities, board members should have access to accurate, relevant and timely information.

The OECD website has a lot of information about corporate governance in member states, as well as containing the OECD Principles. The home page at www.oecd.org links directly to this material through the heading "corporate governance".

3 **The core competencies of company directors**

What competencies should people have if they are to perform effectively as company directors? This beguilingly straightforward question as yet lacks a straightforward answer.

The legal duties, rights and liabilities of directors are well documented in major jurisdictions. Legal commentaries on directors' roles and responsibilities usually emphasise the fiduciary duty to act honestly in good faith for the benefit of all shareholders and, consequently, comment on the importance of independence and personal integrity. Similarly, the requirement to exercise reasonable care, diligence and skill is rehearsed, focusing on the need for appropriate knowledge, experience and skill. But companies are now so disparate in size, complexity and ownership structure that such guidance is, at best, at a high level of abstraction. Neither the legal literature nor the common law provides an answer to the question of what core competencies are necessary for effective company direction.

The descriptive and anecdotal literature of corporate governance lays great emphasis on board procedures, stressing the importance of interpersonal skills if directors are to interact effectively, and of the need for directors to have the moral fibre to take tough-minded decisions with the necessary authority, supplemented by an appropriate amount of business knowledge and experience. Of the theoretical bodies of knowledge, stewardship theory adopts a socio-legal perspective, assuming that directors are capable of fulfilling their fiduciary duties; agency theory assumes that they are not, with each director maximising his or her own personal advantage; and stakeholder theories take a socio-philosophical view of corporations in society. But none addresses the question of what competencies are needed to be an effective company director. Little serious research has been done on defining, measuring and refining such core competencies.

The Institute of Directors study

In 1993–94 the UK's Institute of Directors (IOD), together with Henley Management College, undertook some research. Insights into perceptions of good board-level practice were obtained through interviews with individual directors, focus groups of directors and detailed questionnaires sent to directors and others whose opinions could be significant. The results were claimed to "represent a comprehensive view of good practice drawn from a very broad cross-section of commercial companies in diverse settings ... covering a greatly varied spectrum of corporate size and type, encompassing small firms, private and public companies, and subsidiaries of both UK and foreign-owned companies".

Subsequently, the IOD developed a set of standards for good board practice, based on research and grouped under three headings: organising and running the board; the tasks of the board and indicators of good practice; and building an effective board. Thus the primary focus of the standards was on the activities of the board as a whole. However, the following suggestions are made for the personal qualities required by directors.

Strategic perception and decision-making

Perspective. Rises above the immediate problem or situation and sees the wider issues and implications; relates disparate facts through an ability to perceive all relevant relationships.
Organisational awareness. Is aware of the organisation's strengths and weaknesses and of the impact of the board's decisions upon them.
Strategic awareness. Is sensitive to the interests of shareholders and other interested parties, and to the market, economic, technological and regulatory factors that could affect the organisation's opportunities.
Vision. Is able to produce a clear and consistent picture of the long-term future and the character of the organisation in relation to its environment.
Imagination. Generates and recognises imaginative solutions and innovations.

Judgment. Makes sensible decisions or recommendations based on reasonable assumptions and factual information.

Decisiveness. Shows a readiness to take decisions, make judgments, take action and make commitments.

Change-orientated. Alert and responsive to the need for change. Encourages new initiatives and the implementation of new policies, structures and practices.

Analytical understanding

Information collection. Systematically seeks all possible relevant information for the task from a variety of sources.

Detail consciousness. Insists that sufficiently detailed and reliable information is taken account of and reported as necessary.

Numerical interpretation. Assimilates numerical and statistical information accurately and makes sensible, sound interpretations.

Problem analysis. Identifies problems, transforms and relates information from different sources and identifies possible or actual causes.

Critical faculty. Probes the facts, challenges assumptions, identifies the advantages and disadvantages of proposals, provides counter-arguments and ensures discussions are penetrating.

Communication

Oral communication. Fluent, speaks clearly, audibly and has good diction. Concise, avoids jargon and tailors contents to the audience's needs.

Listening. Listens dispassionately, intently and carefully; key points are recalled and taken into account.

Openness. Is frank and open in his or her communications. Willing to admit errors and shortcomings.

Written communication. Written matter is readily intelligible; ideas and opinions are conveyed clearly and concisely to the reader.

Interacting with others

Co-ordinating. Adopts appropriate interpersonal styles and methods in guiding the board towards task accomplishment. Fosters co-operation and effective teamwork.

Assertiveness. Is assertive and forceful when dealing with others. Ready to take charge of a situation.

Impact. Makes a strong, positive impression on first meeting. Has authority and credibility, establishes rapport quickly.

Persuasiveness. Persuades others to give their agreement and commitment; in face of conflict uses personal influence to achieve compromise and agreement.

Motivating others. Inspires others to achieve goals by ensuring a clear understanding of what needs to be achieved, and by showing commitment, enthusiasm and support.

Sensitivity. Shows an understanding of the feelings and needs of others, and a willingness to provide personal support or to take other actions as appropriate.

Flexibility. Adopts a flexible (but not compliant) style when interacting with others. Takes their views into account and changes position when appropriate.

Board management

Planning. Determines courses of action for self and others. Is competent at establishing priorities and taking account of all relevant contingencies.

Delegating. Allocates decision-making and other tasks to appropriate subordinates and colleagues. Distinguishes between what should be done by others and by self.

Appraising. Evaluates the performance of the board and its members and provides appropriate feedback.

Developing directors. Ensures the development of the skills and personal qualities of fellow directors through training and development related to current and future jobs.

Achieving results

Energy. Shows conspicuous levels of energy, vitality and output.

Achievement and motivation. Sets high goals or standards of performance for self and for others and is dissatisfied with average performance.

Determination. Stays with a position or plan of action until the desired objective is achieved or is no longer reasonably attainable, irrespective of setbacks and obstacles.

Independence. Takes action in which the dominant influence is his or her own convictions rather than other influences.

Risk taking. Is prepared to take action that involves significant risk in order to achieve a desired benefit or advantage.

Business sense. Identifies those opportunities that will increase the organisation's business advantage; selects and exploits those activities that will result in the largest returns.

Resilience. Maintains effectiveness in face of adversity or unfairness. Retains composure when under pressure, and does not become irritable or anxious.

Integrity. Is truthful and trustworthy, can be relied upon to keep his or her word. Does not have double standards and does not compromise on matters of moral principle or the law.

Source: Institute of Directors, 1995

Inevitably, the suggestions above are descriptions of generalised personal qualities that every director needs, rather than core competencies that are necessary to be a successful director on a specific board. They reflect personality attributes, such as independence, determination and the ability to take risk; they do not claim to be core competencies that can be learned, either through formal training or from experience. Others involve moral characteristics, such as integrity and resilience, which again are not core competencies, though they are vital attributes that underlie them. Core competencies are more likely to be contingent on the culture of the specific company and its board, on the industry context, and perhaps on the national culture and company law jurisdiction.

The MTRC project on executive directors' competencies

In 1991 the Hong Kong Mass Transit Railway Company (MTRC) established a project to determine the core competencies of executive directors. These were defined as the competencies critical to success as an executive director of that company. They aimed to identify the high-level discriminators for success as an executive director of MTRC and were derived from in-depth job analysis. The organisation then used these criteria to assess potential executive directors.

The core competencies identified by MTRC were as follows.

Strategic vision and planning

The ability to think independently, originally and proactively; to take a broad cross-functional corporate view. To have vision for the future. To be capable of taking into account and to foresee the implications of important economic, social and political developments. To be able to identify strategic direction for the corporation and develop broad comprehensive strategies, for introducing change or preventing recurrences of problems, which are clearly capable of being translated into management action.

Strategic reasoning skills

To be capable of synthesising and integrating information from a number of sources and to establish hypotheses, theories or a more complete body of related information. To possess strong powers of analysis, and be capable of quickly reading and accurately interpreting large volumes of often technically complex information and data. To be able to apply principles of logic to solve both conceptual and practical problems. To have highly developed critical faculties, capable of objectively discriminating between the relative priorities of strategic issues.

Decision-making

To be able to exercise judgment, bringing to bear all relevant information to arrive at decisions often involving the allocation of fiscal resources. To be capable of deciding action through consensus with others and of taking tough, commercially necessary decisions as well as difficult decisions affecting the welfare of others. To be able to objectively and pragmatically evaluate information and draw sound, logical conclusions even when under pressure and on occasion extreme time constraints.

Team membership and directing skills

To be capable of working effectively and flexibly as a member of a peer-group team, taking charge of the team in crisis where his or her technical expertise is required while at the same time being capable of deferring to other team members as more appropriate leaders in other situations and giving them full support. To be able to provide strategic direction for others and to delegate and empower management to implement appropriate action. To be able to act as an objective overseer of management performance and decisions.

Communication skills

To be able to express ideas clearly and persuasively to both internal and external bodies. To be capable of listening carefully and acting as a sounding board for the chairman and other directors. To have the personality predisposition to be culturally sensitive and capable of creating empathy with a wide range of diverse people. To be a strong negotiator able to remain calm and controlled in often emotional situations and under aggressive questioning. To have good formal presentation skills.

Personal strength and motivation

To have high personal integrity and strong motivation for achievement. To be prepared to stand his or her ground. To have the courage of his or her convictions and yet at the same time be prepared to reach reasonable compromise. Not to be unreasonably stubborn but to be persistent, not to give in to difficulties, and to be dedicated to completing tasks whatever the time or effort required. To be loyal to the corporation and prepared to put the organisation ahead of personal preferences.

Political awareness and networking skills

To be able to initiate and maintain a wide range of contacts in government and political circles. To keep up professional contact. To be capable of commanding respect in the international community. To be diplomatic and demonstrate good social skills. To be politically astute, skilful at lobbying support internally and externally and capable of persuading and influencing individuals of equal or greater status and power.

Professional corporate and commercial understanding

To keep up-to-date with and be able to command professional respect within one's own field of expertise. To have a good understanding of the workings of the corporation as well as a sound grasp of developments in the transport industry world-wide. To be customer-oriented as well as concerned with getting a good deal for the corporation. To be alert to commercial opportunities and sensitive to market movements. To have a good understanding of financial management and the operations of international money markets.

Source: Mass Transit Railway Corporation, Internal Assessment Centre, 1995

4 **Induction checklist for new directors**

Outside directors never know enough about the business to be useful and inside directors always know too much to be independent. So runs one criticism of traditional board practice. Working through the items on this checklist will improve the quality of directors' contributions and reduce the time it takes for them to contribute fully and effectively. Induction exercises for directors will ensure that all board members are fully informed about the company, the business and its financials, the three fundamental areas in which directors need to be conversant and competent. Obviously, directors vary in the extent of their knowledge of the company and its business, but the checklist will provide an *aide-memoire* for both outside and inside directors.

The checklist can be used by chairmen and CEOs planning an induction programme for their board members and by newly appointed directors wanting to brief themselves. It has also proved useful for directors of long standing, by highlighting areas of knowledge and work that they might previously have overlooked.

1 Knowledge of the company

The first broad focus of the induction programme is on the company and its governance. The chairman, other long-serving directors and the company secretary can often be helpful in this regard. If in doubt, it is always wise to seek legal opinion.

Ownership power

In the joint stock limited liability company ownership is the ultimate basis of governance power. What is the actual balance of the equity shareholding and voting power? Has the balance changed in the past and how have the votes been used? How might it change and the voting strength be used in the future? Consider, for example in a family company, what might happen as shares are transferred on succession. Or, in a widely held public company, consider the potential for a merger or hostile bid. What anti-takeover provisions, if any, are in place? How effective might they be?

In a company limited by guarantee, or any other corporate entity governed by its members, how active is the membership in governance matters? Could this situation change in the future? Explore the way that the board communicates with the members and whether there have been any attempts by members to influence corporate affairs. Not-for-profit organisations often seem to generate controversial, even adversarial, activity among their members.

Governance rules, regulations and company law

Study the articles of association and memorandum or corporate rule book. These are the formal documents created on incorporation and updated subject to the approval of the members. Within the constraints of the company law and the listing rules (for a quoted public company), they determine the way the company can be governed. The memorandum, for example, could limit the size of the board, lay down rules for the selection of the board chairman, or define conditions for the meeting and voting of the members. All too often directors are not familiar with the contents of the company's memorandum and are surprised to find themselves constrained in some way, for example in the percentage of members' votes needed to change the capital structure or sell off part of the enterprise.

In a listed public company, be familiar with the listing rules of the stock exchanges on which the company's shares are quoted. Some directors feel that this is a matter that can reasonably be left to the company secretary, share registrar or corporate legal counsel. It is difficult to ask appropriate questions that ensure compliance if you are not familiar with the basic requirements. There is an important distinction between delegation and abdication of responsibility.

Be familiar with the broad scope of the company law of the jurisdiction in which the company is incorporated and has its major bases. Obviously, the detailed requirements of company law vary between Delaware and California, Australia and

Canada, or the UK and France, but there can also be fundamental differences, particularly in the handling of private companies. Companies incorporated in the British Virgin Islands, for example, are not required to have an audit, there is virtually no public filing of documents and the rights of members can be severely limited if they are not also directors.

It is not necessary for a director to be a lawyer or accountant to fulfil such responsibilities, but company law around the world typically expects directors to show the degree of knowledge and skill that a reasonable person would associate with company directorship. In the old days this might not have amounted to very much; today expectations are running high.

Board structure, membership and processes

What is the structure of the board? That is, what is the balance between executive and non-executive directors? In your opinion is this appropriate? Are the outside, non-executive directors independent or do they have some connection with the company, such as being a nominee for a major shareholder or lender, being members of the family of the chairman or CEO, or holding an executive directorship in the past? Such matters could affect your assessment of the position they take on board issues.

Is the board chairmanship separated from the role of chief executive? If not, is there a danger that a single individual dominates the board, and are you able to operate in such a climate? Who are the other board members? Do you know them? If not, some effort to learn about their background, experience and reputation could reinforce your early contributions to board discussions. Meeting individual directors to discuss corporate matters before your first board meeting might help you to discover whether the chemistry of the board is likely to be appropriate for you. Is there a succession plan for key directors and top management? Is there a strategy for development at board level to ensure that the business does not outgrow the board?

How often does the board meet? How long do typical meetings last? What role does the chairman play in board matters? Ask for the agenda and minutes of recent board meetings. Talk to the company secretary about the way the board meetings are run. Does the board operate with committees, an executive committee, audit, remuneration or nominating committees, for example? Find out what you can about the membership, chairmanship and style of these committees. Again study their minutes and discuss with their chairman or the company secretary how they operate.

What information do the directors routinely receive? Ask for all the documentation that was provided for recent meetings. Study the reports and consider the scope of the routine performance data provided. Is it adequate? Does the board have briefings and presentations from non-board senior executives or other experts from time to time? Do the directors meet the auditors periodically?

2 Knowledge of the business

The second focus of this induction checklist is on the business itself. Do you know enough about the business to make an effective contribution? Obviously, this is a reasonable question to ask an outside director who has little or no experience in this particular industry. Interestingly, it is also a pertinent question to put to many executive directors. Expertise and success in a particular function (finance and accounting, perhaps), or high managerial performance in running a division or group company, do not necessarily provide a view of the business as a whole. Indeed, they might have created a narrow window of experience through which the entire corporate business is viewed. This part of the checklist is relevant to all directors.

The basic business processes

Can you outline the fundamental steps in the added-value chain or network of the firm? This is as pertinent a question for directors of a bank, a telecommunications company or an airline, as it is for those of a manufacturing business (although the basic processes are often more difficult to identify). Are you familiar with the major sources of the business inputs, where they come from and who provides them? Within the business processes, which add the value and provide competitive advantage, and which drive the costs? What are the core competencies or capabilities of the business? What is the range of products and services provided by the business? Find out all you can from catalogues, trade literature, customer promotions, trade shows and similar sources of information. Who are the customers? What sectors and markets are served? Pareto's law often applies to products and customers: 80% of the value comes from 20% of the list. Which products and customers form this 20%?

Corporate strategies

Does the firm have a written mission statement or a set of core values? Is there a shared view of the business direction, clearly articulated in strategies, plans and projects? Obtain copies and discuss them with the chairman or CEO. If not, what is the broad direction of the business; what strategies are emergent from recent actions, such as strategies of growth through investment in new product development or through acquisition and divestment? Are there any written policies or management manuals? Again study and discuss them. For example, as far as customers are concerned, are there specific pricing policies and credit policies?

Who are the principal competitors? What competitive advantages and disadvantages do they have, and what strategies are they pursuing? Are there potential new entrants into the market or new technological developments, products or services that might provide alternative competition? Is the business involved in strategic alliances; for example, joint ventures to develop new strategic areas, to supply goods or services, or provide access to distribution channels?

How is strategic change initiated in the firm? Does the board respond to ideas put up by the CEO and senior management, or is the board intimately involved in strategy formulation?

Organisation, management and people

What is the formal organisation structure? Discuss with the CEO and other members of senior management how the organisation works in practice. Form a view of the management culture and style throughout the business: it may differ around the world.

What management control systems are used, for example, for budgetary planning and control, profit centres, performance centres? What management performance measures are used? Are they linked to managerial incentives? Are there employee or senior management share option schemes?

How many employees are there in the various parts of the business? What are the characteristics of the workforce? Are trade unions important and is there a policy towards them? What are the remuneration and other employment policies?

Overall, how would you assess the current position of the business? What needs to be done to maintain and enhance future performance?

3 Knowledge of the financials

The financial aspects of the organisation inevitably feature strongly in typical board discussions.

Study the annual accounts and directors' reports for the past few years. What have been the trends? Consider the trends of key financial ratios, for example: overall performance ratios, such as return on equity and return on investment, and working capital management ratios, such as inventory turnover rates, liquidity ratios, debt collection rates. Does the company measure shareholder added value?

Trends are likely to convey more information than the actual ratios for the business itself, whereas the financial ratios at a point in time can be useful for cross-industry comparisons. What are the projections for these financial criteria? How does the financial position of the company compare with that of its principal competitors?

Review the financial performance of parts of the business, such as product or geographical divisions or subsidiary companies. Review the criteria used in investment project appraisals.

How is the company financed? What is the financial structure? What implications might the debt/equity ratio have for the future? For example, what might be the effect of a significant change in interest rates given this gearing or leverage?

Who are the auditors? Ask to see any management letter written after the last audit discussing issues that arose during the audit.

4 Expectations on appointment

All directors should discuss with the chairman what is expected of their directorship before accepting nomination. Consequently, a crucial part of any induction briefing should review the expectations of the chairman and the other directors.

Is a specific role expected of you? Was there a special reason, perhaps, for your nomination to the board? For example, did it reflect your particular knowledge in some area, or special skills or experience you could bring to board discussions, or a special channel of communication and information you could provide? Or was the nomination made because of your overall experience and potential contribution to all aspects of the board's work? Are you capable of fulfilling these expectations? If not, what other information, knowledge or skill will you need to obtain?

How much time do they expect you to give to the board, its committees and other aspects of the company's affairs? This should cover not only attendance at regular meetings, but also the time needed for briefings and discussions, visits within the company and preparation. Outside directors will have to ensure that this is compatible with other demands on their time. Executive directors will need to harmonise these expectations and their directorial responsibilities with the duties required under their contract of employment with the company.

Although all directors have the right to be informed on all board matters, confirm that you will have appropriate access to the information you require. This should cover not only formal board papers, but also the right to seek additional information if necessary. Are you able to talk to the managers? If so, under what circumstances?

Last, but not least, review the details of the contractual relationship between you and the company. What are the terms of appointment as a director? Is there a written contract or a formal letter of appointment from the chairman? Length of appointment? Terms and likelihood of reappointment? Basis of the remuneration package and manner of review? Terms of any directors' and officers' indemnity insurance (particularly important in the increasingly litigious climate facing directors in many parts of the world)?

Finally, a word of encouragement. All directors, without exception, face a challenge as they join a new board. Effective board membership involves a learning experience. It should start well before the director attends the first board meeting and should continue during all the rest. The successful director is the one who can say, "Aha! I hadn't realised that, now I understand," not once but continuously, throughout his or her service on the board.

5 **Effectiveness checklist for boards**

There is no board of directors or governing body in the world which, if the members think about it, cannot improve its effectiveness. That is the belief behind this checklist of opportunities. All too readily board members grow old together. Often the business outgrows the board. Few boards take a rigorous look at themselves. A review of board effectiveness can be a salutary experience, but it can lead to important changes.

A board review involves a comprehensive, tough-minded look at the board and its activities. The aim is to explore the board's structure, style and processes in the light of changing company needs, to highlight potential problems for the future and provide the basis for improving effectiveness today.

Such a review needs the enthusiastic support and co-operation of all members if it is to succeed. It can be led by the board chairman, one of the outside directors, an ad-hoc board committee or someone with suitable experience from outside the board. Obviously, it is a highly confidential activity.

The review process involves marshalling a lot of information about the underlying governance power-base in the company, the board structure and its members, and the way the board and its committees work, including the information they receive and the way they allocate their time. Various ideas, issues and opinions will then emerge. Alternatives can be developed and evaluated. In due course the options can be discussed by the directors, leading eventually to a strategy for the development of the board and the way it works. The process needs to be taken step by step.

1 Set the board review in the context of the company's business strategy

As companies grow in complexity, diversity and size, it seems obvious that their boards ought also to evolve to reflect such changes. Unfortunately, this is not always the case. If, for example, the company's strategy involves new technologies, markets or international locations, if it is developing new strategic alliance or acquisition strategies, or if its plans call for different global financing strategies such as the use of derivatives, it is essential that among the board members are those able to understand the issues and, in due course, monitor executive management's performance. Thus the first step towards creating a strategy for board development is to consider the implications at board level of the corporate business strategy as a whole. The board review must be in line with, and preferably part of, the company's overall business strategy.

2 Review the overall governance situation

This can be particularly important, yet easily overlooked. The key question is: who has ultimate power over the company and might this change over the strategic time horizon of the board review? If so, what would be the implications for governance and the board? For example, in a public listed company, what are the prospects of a change of ownership through a friendly or hostile bid? In a company with a dominant shareholder, what might happen to the board if this shareholding changed hands? In a family firm, how might the balance of power change on succession? It is important not only to know precisely the current ownership of the voting equity but also to consider possible future scenarios. Detailed knowledge of the company's articles of association is important as well. There may be unexpected clauses about percentages of shareholder votes needed to approve various strategic changes, such as introducing new capital or divesting part of the business.

3 Consider relevant external factors

This means looking at the context in which the governance of the company must operate over the time horizon of the review. Are there any legal, political or societal factors that could affect the governance of the company? Examples include possible changes to company legislation in any of the countries in which the company operates, new regulations from the European Union about worker representation in strategic decision-making, the imposition of new disclosure requirements in stock exchange listing rules, or the possible effects of a change of government. Any plans for developing the board must take account of the changing governance environment.

4 Review board structure

Consider the size of the board. Is it appropriate for the task that needs to be done? There may be a case for additional members; or the board may have grown too big. Consider the structure of the board. Is the balance between executive and non-executive members appropriate? This issue needs to be reviewed along with the identification of board style and the way the members work together. Are enough of the non-executive directors genuinely independent? This means ensuring that the independent outside directors have no relationships with the company that could affect the exercise of genuinely objective judgment. Are the posts of chairman of the board and chief executive separate? Is the present arrangement the most satisfactory for the future?

5 Identify board style

Consider how the board's work has evolved in recent years. Reflect on the effects of changes of chairman and other members. Review the way the directors work together. Is this a genuinely professional board style or are there elements of rubber-stamp, representative or country-club boards? What changes might be necessary to meet different circumstances in the future?

6 Review board membership and the roles directors play, formulate succession plans

Consider the detailed membership of the board. Summarise the résumé of each director. Does the board have the balance of knowledge, skills and experience that will be needed for the planned future of the company? Look at the age profile of members. How many directors will retire over the review's time horizon? What is the probability of any directors resigning? Develop succession plans for both executive and non-executive directors. Boards should always have a portfolio of potential non-executive directors who could be considered for board appointment, and the management development plans for senior executive staff should also include their potential as directors. (See also Appendix 3.)

7 Consider director development and training

As much attention should be given to director development and training as is given to management development and training, but it seldom is. Directors all too readily assume that, having reached the board, they must have the experience to perform as directors. But governance, the work of the board, is not the same as management. It calls for additional knowledge and different skills. Consider the development needs of each director. This could involve a carefully developed induction or updating programme on the company and its work, or experiential development, such as chairing a board task force or one of the board committees; or it might be achieved through participation in the growing number of director-level courses and programmes around the world.

8 Achieving greater efficiency: review directors' time and information

How does the board spend its time? Is this the most effective use of one of the most valuable resources the company has? Does the board delegate some of its work to board committees? Are these as effective as they could be? This information can be extracted from an analysis of the agenda and minutes of the board and its committees, and by discussing the issue with each director. Similarly, review the nature, extent and adequacy of the information available to directors. How could the routine board papers be improved? Can directors readily obtain the additional information they want? Do the outside directors have access to management information? Is there a case for board-level briefings to keep directors up-to-date and provide the context for board-level discussions? What ideas does each director have for improvement in the information process?

9 Achieving greater effectiveness: better strategy formulation and policymaking

Review the board's contribution to the performance roles of strategy formulation and policymaking. Is adequate time devoted to this part of the board's responsibilities? Are all board members adequately informed about strategic matters? Is there a shared vision and understanding of the company's core values and competencies among all the directors? Are there any differences of view as to the strategic direction of the firm? Are the policy guidelines laid down by the board adequate for management decision-making and balancing control and freedom appropriately? What ideas do directors have for improvement?

10 Achieving greater effectiveness: better executive supervision and accountability

Turning to the conformance roles of the board, do the directors adequately monitor and supervise executive management? Is the feedback of information relevant and timely? How might the process be improved? Seek the opinions of all directors and senior managers, as well as the auditors and others in a position to take a view on board activities. Is the board providing appropriate accountability to all those with a legitimate claim to be informed? Does this include a commitment to employees, customers and suppliers, or does the board accept a responsibility only to be accountable to the shareholders? Is this responsibility adequately fulfilled? Consider the published report, other communications and meetings with the members, analysts and the media. What ideas are there for improvement?

11 Develop and agree the strategy for board development

From the mass of hard data, opinion and ideas for improvement that have been gathered, marshal the facts, identify alternatives and articulate their implications. Develop a report for discussion by the board. Such a review might well take place as part of a strategy seminar, rather than in a formal board meeting, to encourage open discussion and creativity. Move towards forming a strategy for developing the board. This could include planned changes to board size, structure or membership, new sources and forms of providing information, other uses of directors' time, such as a new committee structure, different formats for board meetings, or calling on some directors to commit different amounts of time to their board duties. Agree the strategy, ensuring that it is consistent with, indeed part of, the overall business strategy.

12 Determine action plans and projects

Lastly, develop the procedures, plans and projects that will turn the strategy into realised change. Ensure commitment from all those involved. Get feedback periodically to confirm that the changes are taking place as planned and that the results are as expected. Continue the strategic review and change programme as part of the board's constant learning and relearning process.

6 A charter for an audit committee

An audit committee needs to have clear terms of reference, which define its purpose, authority, membership and chairmanship; the frequency of and attendance at meetings; and its duties. The following charter, adapted to the specific governance circumstances in a company, can provide a basis for the development of an audit committee.

Purpose

The audit committee is a standing committee of the board of directors, providing a board-level link between the independent external auditors and the board. Its functions include:

- advising the board on the systems of internal management control and on matters of internal audit;
- liaising with the external auditors and reporting to the board on the audit process and on any audit issues;
- reviewing financial information to be provided to shareholders and others;
- advising the board on matters of board accountability.

Authority

The audit committee has the power to authorise and conduct whatever meetings, interviews or investigations it deems necessary. The audit committee may seek information directly from any company employee, although normally this should be done with the knowledge of the CEO or finance director. The head of the internal audit function reports directly to the chairman of the audit committee. The committee may obtain independent accounting, legal or other professional advice in pursuit of its responsibilities.

Membership

The audit committee shall consist of not less than three and not more than five independent non-executive (outside) directors, the quorum being two. At least one member should have significant, recent and relevant financial experience.

Chairmanship

The chairman of the audit committee shall be appointed by the board.

Meeting frequency

The audit committee shall meet whenever it deems necessary with a minimum of three times a year (typically before, during and at the conclusion of the external audit process). The external auditors may also request a meeting with the audit committee if they deem it necessary.

Meeting participation

Typically, the finance director (or chief financial officer), the internal auditor and a representative of the external auditors will attend meetings of the audit committee. Other executive directors or members of management may be asked to attend if necessary. The audit committee may meet separately with the external auditor, the internal auditor, other directors or members of management should they have matters they wish to raise privately with the committee. At least once a year, the audit committee will meet with the external auditor without any members of management being present. The external auditors will also meet with the entire board at least once a year and be available to answer questions at meetings of the shareholders.

Duties

The responsibilities of the audit committee include the following duties.

1 Monitoring the integrity of the company's financial statements.

2 Reviewing the company's internal financial control and risk management systems.

3 Monitoring and evaluating the effectiveness of the company's internal audit function.

4 Liaison between the external auditor, the internal auditor and the board as a whole.

5 Advising the board on the appointment, reappointment, resignation or replacement of the external auditor.

6 Ensuring the independence of the external auditor, reviewing the extent of non-audit work undertaken by the external auditor and the fees involved.

7 Review of the audit fees and advising the board accordingly.

8 Considering the scope of the work and plans of the external audit.

9 Considering the scope of the work and plans of the internal audit. Supervising the work of the head of the internal audit function, including the setting of policies, procedures and plans, the budgeting of resources, the remuneration and performance of staff, the regular monitoring of results and the overall effectiveness of the function.

10 Ensuring that the activities of the external and internal auditors are co-ordinated, avoiding both duplication and incomplete coverage.

11 Review of the appointment, performance, remuneration and replacement or dismissal of the head of the internal audit function, ensuring continuing independence of the internal audit function from undue managerial influence.

12 Reviewing with the external and internal auditors and advising the board on the adequacy of the company's internal control systems, security of physical assets and protection of information.

13 Reviewing with the external and internal auditors and advising the board on the conduct of the external audit, particularly any important findings or matters raised, usually contained in the auditor's management letter, with management's response. Reporting any significant changes to the reporting of financial results or to procedures and management controls that resulted.

14 Reviewing with the external and internal auditors and advising the board on the company's financial statements (interim and annual) prior to publication, the auditor's report to the shareholders, any changes to accounting policies, material issues arising in or from the financial statements; and compliance with accounting standards, company law (and if appropriate stock exchange) reporting requirements and corporate governance codes of good practice.

15 Review of any other published information, such as the directors' report, and ensuring that it is consistent with the audited financial statements.

16 Reviewing the exposure of the company to risk and any matters that might have a material effect on the company's financial position, including any matters raised by company regulators or stock exchange listing committees.

17 Reviewing annually the charter of the audit committee and advising the chairman of the board if changes are necessary.

18 Developing and implementing policy on the engagement of the external auditor to supply non-audit services in the light of relevant ethical guidelines.

7 Sources of information

Corporate governance organisations

Boardseat – US director search and research
www.boardseat.com
Centre for International Private Enterprise
www.cipe.org
Commonwealth Business Council
www.cbc.to
Corporate governance portal
www.corpgov.net
Corporate monitoring, Mark Latham
www.corpmon.com
European Corporate Governance Institute
www.ecgi.org
Financial Reporting Council (UK)
www.frc.org.uk
Global Corporate Governance Network
www.gcgf.org
Global Reporting Initiative
www.globalreporting.org

Online resources, journals and newsletters

Boardroom (Canadian journal)
www.boardroomnews.com
Boardroom Insider
www.boardroominsider.com
Chartered Secretary
www.charteredsecretary.net
The Corporate Library
www.thecorporatelibrary.com
Corporate Governance
www.abgweb.com
Corporate Governance: An International Review
www.blackwellpublishing.com

Corporate Governance: International Journal of Effective Board Performance
www.emerald-library.com

The Corporate Governance Network
www.corpgov.net

Corporate Governance Newsletter, British Accounting Association
www.baacgsig.qub.ac.uk

Corporate Governance Newsletter
www.management-audit.com

The Economist – archive, briefings
www.economist.com

European Corporate Governance Institute, Belgium
www.ecgi.org

Governance – monthly newsletter, UK
www.governance.co.uk

Robert A.G. Monks online articles and books
www.ragm.com

Wall Street Journal
www.wsj.com

Professional bodies relevant to corporate governance

American Accounting Association
www.rutgers.edu/accounting/raw/aaa

American Institute of Certified Public Accountants
www.aicpa.org

Australian Accounting Research Foundation
www.aarf.asn.au

Australian Institute of Company Directors
www.companydirectors.com.au

British Accounting Association – corporate governance special interest group
www.baacgsig.qub.ac.uk

Canadian Institute of Chartered Accountants – Joint Committee on Corporate Governance
www.cica.ca

Conference Board, US (corporate governance area)
www.conference-board.org

Council of Institutional Investors
www.cii.org

European Corporate Governance Institute
www.ecgi.org

Institute of Chartered Secretaries and Administrators
www.icsa.org.uk

Institute of Corporate Directors, Canada
www.icd.ca

Institute of Directors in New Zealand
www.iod.org.nz

Institute of Directors of South Africa
www.iodsa.co.za

Institute of Directors, UK
www.iod.com

Russian Institute of Directors
www.rid.ru

Securities and Exchange Commission, US
www.sec.gov

Institute of Chartered Accountants in England and Wales
www.icaew.co.uk

National Association of Corporate Directors, US
www.nacdonline.org

National Association of Security Dealers, US – advice for audit
committee members
www.nasd.com

Organisation for Economic Co-operation and Development
www.oecd.org

World Bank
www.worldbank.org

World Business Council for Sustainable Development
www.wbcsd.ch

8 Recommended reading

Berle, A. and Means, G., *The Modern Corporation and Private Property*, Macmillan, New York, 1932. (The first and most frequently quoted study of corporate governance, though they did not use that phrase.)

Brancato, C.K., *Institutional Investors and Corporate Governance: Best Practices for Increasing Corporate Value*, The Conference Board and McGraw-Hill, New York, 1997.

Cadbury, A., *Corporate Governance and Chairmanship: A Personal View*, Oxford University Press, Oxford, 2002.

Carver, J., *Corporate Boards that Create Value*, Jossey-Bass, San Francisco, 2002.

Charkham, J., *Keeping Good Company: A Study of Corporate Governance in Five Countries*, Oxford University Press, Oxford, 1994.

Charkham, J. and Simpson, A., *Fair Shares: The Future of Shareholder Power and Responsibility*, Oxford University Press, Oxford, 1999.

Demb, A. and Neubauer, F., *The Corporate Board: Confronting the Paradoxes*, Oxford University Press, New York, 1992.

Dunne, P., *Running Board Meetings: Tips and Techniques for Getting the Best From Them*, 2nd edition, Kogan Page, London, 1999.

Dunne, P., *Directors' Dilemmas: Tips and Techniques for Dealing with Day-to-day Problems*, Kogan Page, London, 2000.

Garratt, B., *The Fish Rots from the Head: The Crisis in Our Boardrooms: Developing the Crucial Skills of the Competent Director*, Profile Books, London, 1997.

Gugler, K. (ed.), *Corporate Governance and Economic Performance*, Oxford University Press, Oxford, 2001.

Hilmer, F.G. (chairman), *Strictly Boardroom: Improving Governance to Enrich Company Performance*, a study facilitated by the Sydney Institute; Information Australia, Melbourne, Australia, 1993.

Hutton, W. and others, *Stakeholding and its Critics*, IEA Health and Welfare Unit, 2 North Street, London SW1P 3LB, 1997.

Institute of Chartered Accountants in England and Wales,
Audit Faculty, *Audit Committees: A Framework for
Assessment*, London, May 1997.

Keasey, K., Thompson, S. and Wright, M., *Corporate
Governance: Economic and Financial Issues*, Oxford
University Press, Oxford, 1997.

Learmount, S., *Corporate Governance: What Can Be Learned
from Japan?*, Oxford University Press, Oxford, 2002.

Lorsch, J.W. and MacIver, E., *Pawns or Potentates: The Reality of
America's Corporate Boards*, Harvard Business School Press,
Boston, MA, 1989.

McCahery, J.A., Moerland, P., Raaijmakers, T. and Renneboog,
L., *Corporate Governance Regimes: Convergence and
Diversity*, Oxford University Press, Oxford, 2002.

Millstein, I.M. and Katsh, S.M., *The Limits of Corporate Power:
Existing Constraints on the Exercise of Corporate Discretion*,
Collier-Macmillan, New York, 1981.

Monks, R.A.G. and Minow, N., *Corporate Governance*,
Blackwell, Oxford, 1994.

Monks, R.A.G., *The Emperor's Nightingale: How the emerging
dynamics of corporate complexity will restore integrity to
economic life in the new Millennium*, Capstone, Oxford, 1998.

Monks, R.A.G., *The New Global Investors: How Shareowners can
Unlock Sustainable Prosperity Worldwide*, Capstone
Publishing (Wiley), Oxford, 2001.

O'Sullivan, M.A., *Contests for Corporate Control: Corporate
Governance and Economic Performance in the United States
and Germany*, Oxford University Press, Oxford, 2000.

Stiles, P. and Taylor, B., *Boards at Work: How Directors View
Their Roles and Responsibilities*, Oxford University Press,
Oxford, 2001.

Sykes, A., *Capitalism for Tomorrow: Reuniting Ownership and
Control*, Capstone Publishing, Oxford, 2000.

Tricker, R.I., *Corporate Governance*, Gower, Aldershot, 1984.
(The first book to use the phrase "corporate governance" in
its title.)

Tricker R.I., *Corporate Governance*, in *The History of
Management Thought* series, Ashgate Publishing, Gower
Press, Aldershot, 2000.

Turnbull, S., *A New Way to Govern*, download from
www.neweconomics.org

Ward, R.D., *21st Century Corporate Board*, Wiley, New York,
1997.

Wheeler, D. and Sillanpää, M., *The Stakeholder Corporation: A
Blueprint for Maximizing Stakeholder Value* (with foreword
by Anita Roddick, founder of The Body Shop), Pitman
Publishing, London, 1997.